The Inner Work

The Inner Work

An Invitation to True Freedom
and Lasting Happiness

The Yoga Couple
Mat & Ash

~ Dedication ~

First and foremost, we dedicate this work to The Divine Creator
that is the Source of All That Is.

And to all our teachers along the way.

Jesus Christ

Krishna

Siddartha Guatama Buddha

Paramahansa Yogananda

Swami Sri Yukteswar

Lahiri Mahasaya

Mahavatar Babaji

David R. Hawkins

Ramakrishna

Ramana Maharshi

Vivekananda

Maharaj-ji

Ram Dass

Eckhart Tolle

Alan Watts

Michael Bernard Beckwith

Carl Jung

Michael Singer

Neale Donald Walsch

Table of Contents

PART IV — A New Paradigm

Message from the Authors

With a book such as this, it is important for us to clarify that by all means this book is meant for us as much as it is for you—we're reading too in a sense. We humbly bring this message forward in hopes that *The Inner Work* may bring you the same utter satisfaction and joy it has brought us.

The Inner Work is for those who are ready to understand themselves on a deeper level and are yearning for true freedom and lasting happiness. It is especially for those who have read countless books on self-improvement and spirituality, but have yet to make lasting progress. No matter where you are in your journey, this book will help you to acknowledge and overcome the obstacles which prevent you from experiencing optimal states of existence.

To be truly liberated and happy, we have found that the practices shared within these pages must be applied *consistently with conscious effort* in order to prove effective. There is no one-and-done prescription here. All true healing and change must come from an inner transformation of the soul by shedding our old, limiting self in order to embrace our greater destiny. This may bring about lifestyle changes that will reflect the *Inner Work* being done.

It is important to understand that the truth of our joy is not something that has to be learned, gained, or acquired, but rather something we *remember* and *awaken to*. The fullness of our potential is already there and waiting, right now, we just have to do our *Inner Work* to *reveal* it. And for most of us, time will prove to be the greatest gift throughout the healing journey. It is with the sincerest love and humility that the truths within this book will help you in your spiritual awakening and return *home* to true freedom and lasting happiness.

You are always being guided and are never alone.
Everything is unfolding in perfect timing.
You are exactly where you are supposed to be.
All is love. All is Divine. All is perfect.
The answers are here.
Now.

Trigger Warning

A caveat to be aware of: know that more than likely this book will trigger you—this is to be expected and is actually an opportunity and invitation to heal. Become curious about your resistances and their origins and have the courage to lean into them, for your freedom is just beyond the boundaries of your discomfort.

This book is specifically written for anyone who is ready to give up their suffering and move from victim mentality into self-accountability. This stage of healing is not for everyone. There is a healthy time and a place for every *seemingly* negative emotion, such as anger or blame. You can stay there as long as you'd like. Only pick up this book if you are truly ready to move on, as the words within these pages will cause more harm than good without your conscious agreement to hear its motivational messages.

This is a nondenominational spiritual book, not a psychology or medical book, which pulls from a diverse plethora of religious and non-religious sources, including Mystic Christianity, Hinduism, Buddhism, and many more. If you have experienced any religious trauma, know this is a safe space for you to take what spiritual truth serves you and leave behind what doesn't. Your path is yours to forge. There are many rivers that lead to the same sea.

Lastly, this book is for all humans who want to be happy. All genders, races, religions, ethnicities, ages, and personal identifications can equally benefit from the truths shared inside *The Inner Work*. You are loved and perfect exactly as you are. You deserve to be happy and free.

You're Invited to a FREE
Inner Work Online Challenge

Includes BONUS videos and actionable growth activities!

Reading The Inner Work is a profound step in your self-healing journey. To support you in *doing* your Inner Work rather than just reading about it, we have designed a free interactive challenge to accompany your daily reading.

What's included in The Inner Work challenge:

- Inner Work Yoga Classes: Emotions are stored in the body. Learn how to somatically release stuck emotions through yoga, breathwork, and energy clearing practices. Each class is specifically designed to help address the themes of consciousness that you will learn in this book.

- Self-reflection activities: Receive actionable practices, guided meditations, journal prompts, podcast recordings, and Inner Work processes in your inbox.

- Exclusive Reader Community: Join our private online group to ask questions, share, and reflect with other Inner Workers.

By committing to The Inner Work Challenge, you're not just reading a book; you're actively integrating what you are learning and transforming yourself from the inside out

Answer The Call and Unlock This Free Gift:

theinnerwork.com/challenge

PART I

The Human Experience

Chapter 1

Introduction to *The Inner Work*

"The hero's journey is inside of you;
tear off the veils and open the mystery of yourself."
- Joseph Campbell

Welcome to the greatest adventure of your life—the journey back to your true Self—the embodiment of pure love, true freedom, and lasting happiness. The path is simple, yet many find it to be the most challenging of all. This, however, is entirely up to you and your own willingness to surrender resistance, as it is only through the *releasing* of unhealed wounds within your consciousness that you can *remember* the true peace, unconditional love, and eternal joy waiting to be revealed within you.

This shift out of the old and into a new paradigm of true freedom and lasting happiness can transform your current life to heaven on earth. For in this state of consciousness, there is no longer anything wrong or out of place. All is love. All is Divine. All is perfect. It is the realization of ecstatic bliss and serenity that all great teachers have been pointing humanity to. For all notable spiritual texts, from the ancient *Vedas* to the parables of Jesus, tell us that we were intended to enjoy eternal peace, unperturbed by the ever-changing world. And you have access to it all, right now.

> *"For behold, the Kingdom of Heaven is within you."*
> *- Holy Bible, Luke 17:21*

The standards we have accepted regarding our freedom and happiness are simply that—accepted. Meaning they are not being forced or applied from outside of us. They are self-created through our consciousness, and therefore can be self-edited or replaced entirely. We can change and mold our experience of life to be whatever we desire. Nothing is being withheld. There is no shortage of perspectives.

The first step is simply believing you are worthy of all which you are seeking. You were born to be happy and free! We all were. It doesn't matter what your life looks like right now. You always were, and always will be, worthy of experiencing infinite love, joy, and freedom. Understand, though, that no one can give this to you —only you can. *The Inner Work* is a divine, solo mission to actualize your true Self. Only you can realize the truth of who you really are. Only you can be your Self.

> *"Today you are you. That is truer than true.*
> *There is no one alive who is you-er than you."*
> *- Dr. Seuss*

And while you must actualize your potential alone, we can promise you that the outcome will be worth whatever the cost. You will have help and guidance along the way in this journey of life. Your prayers and intentions will always be answered the instant you submit them. Still, ultimately you must have the eyes to see, the ears to hear, and the courage to accept the truth when it reveals itself to you.

You must decide what life you want to live—the life of your *not-self* or the one of your *true-Self*. You must choose. In fact, you *are* choosing, in each and every moment, whether you are conscious of it or not. When faced with the unknown, you must have the willingness to let go of the way you've been living in order to enjoy the life you've always dreamt of. Don't let the internal shackles of limitation and suffering remain comfortable and acceptable to you.

You are a very special being with such a magnificent purpose. You are needed, wanted, seen, understood, accepted, and completely loved. Infinite possibilities are available to you. This *is* the life you dream of having—you just haven't realized it yet. There is nothing out of place, missing, or wrong. It's all here, waiting for you to see it. The destination is no more beautiful than the journey. In truth, there is nowhere else to go. *Now* is the only time to start remembering.

Finding Happiness

"Nobody can hurt me without my permission."
- Mahatma Gandhi

Although the current world paradigm has entrained society to believe in a reality of struggle, the truth is actually effortless. And therefore, so is love, happiness, and internal freedom. The inability to access or maintain the more optimal states of experience in our everyday lives is actually due to one simple factor, our general lack of understanding regarding human consciousness. For it is **consciousness** that is the very *essence of life,* and it is our **theme of consciousness** that determines the quality of our existence. Thus how we experience our lives each and every day has little to do with other people, circumstances or conditions, and has everything to do with what's going on *inside* us.

There is a reason why specific issues continue to resurface no matter how many times we feel we have resolved them. These energetic imprints, or patterns of similar situations, people, challenges, circumstances, thoughts, and feelings, are all clues to an underlying theme of consciousness, which our soul is begging us to break free from. In a sense, no matter where we go or what we do, we always bring our problems with us, like a shadow. This is because all struggle with life is intrinsically rooted in our own consciousness and could never be caused by something or someone outside ourselves.

> *"Everything can be taken from a man but one thing;*
> *the last of human freedoms—to choose one's*
> *attitude in any given set of circumstances..."*
> *- Viktor Frankl (Holocaust survivor)*

The amount of suffering or satisfaction we experience daily is *completely* dependent on our current state of consciousness, which we can heal, transform, and evolve at any time. True freedom and lasting happiness are realized through the *internal* transcendence of wounded themes of consciousness. Unfortunately, not understanding this powerful truth has caused the vast majority of us to tirelessly strive to attain happiness *externally*.

Whether it be through seeking accolades such as accumulating wealth, taking exotic trips, becoming famous, earning titles and ranks within our careers, or fantasizing about the ideal relationship, all searches ultimately stem from the root desire to be loved, happy, and free. And while success, relationships, and achievements can absolutely be fulfilling experiences for the soul, in and of themselves, they do not have the power to *give* us our desired joy. Hence we have reports of many wealthy and famous figures throughout history publicly sharing the realization that even at the top, loneliness and sadness prevail as there is still a missing piece to the puzzle.

"Happiness does not come from the consumption of things."
- Thich Nhat Hanh

The roller coaster of pleasure and pain, the high of achieving goals, and the "come-down" when the elation passes can cause our inner pendulum to swing in the opposite direction in rebellion or disappointment with life. Thus the idea of escaping "the system" can become just as enticing as the desire to conquer it. Attachment to detachment, non-participation, and the fantasy of getting out of the rat race, are just the other side of the same coin. It's all a part of the quest to *acquire* the happiness and freedom we know we deserve.

The truth is, it doesn't matter which side of the pendulum we are on; all attachments and aversions keep us focused *outside* of ourselves. Happiness is not something that can be attained through ideal conditions nor in the escaping of obligations. But rather, happiness is something that we *become* through the transformation of our consciousness. The desire to get someplace else will only keep us stuck in a perpetual cycle of *wanting* happiness rather than *actualizing* it.

The Chase

The illusion is that the closer we move toward our goals and aspirations, regardless of what they are, the closer we feel we will be to the horizon of our freedom and joy. The definition of a horizon, however, is "the limit of perception." There is no actual line at the edge of the earth for the sun to set behind, just as there is no actual milestone, experience, place, or person which can give us our happiness. Therefore, no matter the speed at which we pursue the horizons of our *wanting*, the horizon will continue to move farther away. Because even when we do successfully acquire the object of our desires, we are ultimately still left to face the mundane frustrations of everyday life.

Circumstances inevitably change, people let us down, obligations arise, challenges surface, and life doesn't always go the way we planned. We innocently believe that when we arrive at happiness, we will finally be able to escape these daily struggles. But without actually healing the root of our dissatisfaction with life and evolving our consciousness, our problems will only continue to resurface again in *new forms*, no matter where we go or what we do.

This fragile mentality mistakes happiness, freedom, inner peace, and love as *things* that can be given or taken away from us in any instant. When someone says something we don't like, inner peace is replaced with worry or defensiveness. If someone falls short of our expectations, joy is replaced with disappointment. If obligations arise, we are filled with resistance. If someone interrupts us, we are triggered with impatience. The result of this externally focused perspective is that we have allowed circumstances and other people to bestow good or bad emotions upon us, wrongly accrediting them as the givers or thieves of our joy. However, both favorable and unfavorable emotions are neither the result of conditions or other people's actions; they are the direct result of which theme of consciousness we are living in and our chosen response *to* our life's circumstances.

Introduction to the Themes of Consciousness

Scientific discovery has now revealed that everything in our universe, including human thoughts and emotions, is composed of vibrating energy, each unique and varying in the calibration of frequency. Themes of consciousness reflect these varying frequencies, which are universal to humanity and represent the overall quality of experience each of us is having from our vantage point. We can think of themes of consciousness as the lenses through which we view reality. Thus the frequency we are in, or theme of consciousness our soul is occupying, dictates our levels of suffering, pain, joy, love, peace, and overall level of satisfaction in everyday life.

The Themes of Consciousness

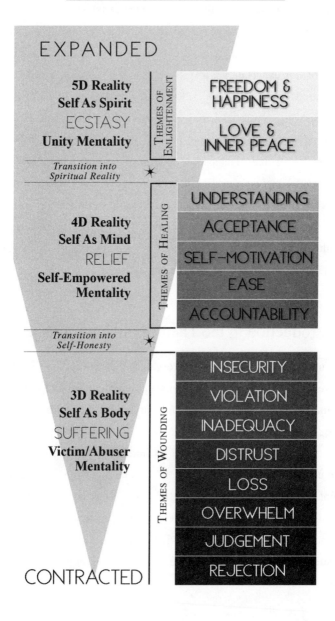

EXPANDED

5D Reality **Self As Spirit** ECSTASY **Unity Mentality**	THEMES OF ENLIGHTENMENT	FREEDOM & HAPPINESS
		LOVE & INNER PEACE
Transition into Spiritual Reality ✶		
4D Reality **Self As Mind** RELIEF **Self-Empowered Mentality**	THEMES OF HEALING	UNDERSTANDING
		ACCEPTANCE
		SELF–MOTIVATION
		EASE
		ACCOUNTABILITY
Transition into Self-Honesty ✶		
3D Reality **Self As Body** SUFFERING **Victim/Abuser Mentality**	THEMES OF WOUNDING	INSECURITY
		VIOLATION
		INADEQUACY
		DISTRUST
		LOSS
		OVERWHELM
		JUDGEMENT
		REJECTION

CONTRACTED

In the second half of this book, we will be exploring in detail how each theme manifests, how to identify their patterns we may find ourselves stuck in, and how to transcend them. We will also reveal how to consciously transition into the liberating themes of love, inner peace, true freedom and lasting happiness forevermore. For now, we want to begin to simply build awareness and familiarity with the themes by showing their variations and progression, as we will be referring to them throughout our journey together.

The first thing to note when looking at the themes of consciousness is that the wound of rejection represents the most cut off from our true Self, whereas true freedom and lasting happiness represent the most unified and Self-realized. Put another way, rejection represents the most lacking, suffering-filled, and painful frequency we could experience, while the theme of true freedom and lasting happiness represents the release of all suffering, making it the most joyful and liberating frequency we could embody. Therefore we could think of the themes of consciousness as an evolution of lovingness and reflective of degrees of happiness and inner freedom.

Most of us will find that we are on a spectrum of consciousness and will have some unhealed wounds still within us while also experiencing themes of healing and enlightenment from time to time. This is to be expected and part of being human. Our anatomy of consciousness is both unique to us and ever fluctuating as we are all energetic beings constantly navigating and responding to the various frequencies we encounter throughout our lives.

SPECTRUM OF CONSCIOUSNESS

0 = NEVER | 1= RARELY | 2 = SOMETIMES | 3= OFTEN | 4 = CONSISTENTLY

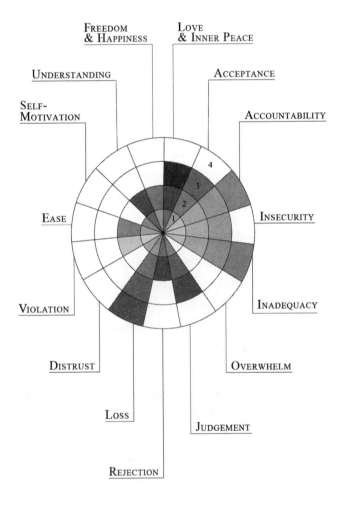

Example of an individual's current spectrum of consciousness

Process of Awakening

This is *The Inner Work*—the removing of all obstacles which stand in the way of our rightful inner peace, freedom, and joy. And luckily, the only obstacle we encounter along this journey is... *ourselves*. It is all within our own control to evolve our consciousness and to transcend our limiting programs. It's only a question of willingness to surrender and receive the goodness that is innately a part of us. Everything we are seeking outside of ourselves is actually already resting in the palms of our own hands.

All resistance to accepting and enjoying deep happiness and fulfillment in our lives ultimately stems from a wounded theme of consciousness. A theme that we innocently inherited at some point along our journey. Through repeated beliefs, thoughts, emotions, and finally, in our words and actions, this limited version of our potential becomes our sense of *who we are*. We then eventually find ourselves stuck in a groove, a pattern of life that we begin to accept as "just the way things are." Luckily, it is completely possible to realign every aspect of our lives back to infinite peace —it is only a matter of looking *within* ourselves and becoming Self-aware.

"Who looks outside, dreams;
who looks inside, awakes–"
- Carl Jung

Chapter 2

Compassion for Ourselves & Others Along the Journey

"The desire to know your own soul will end all other desires."

- Rumi

Regardless of how you feel about yourself or your life right now, it's essential to understand that if your perspective isn't rooted in unconditional love, it is not the truth of your full potential. It's a subjective perspective you are temporarily experiencing that is coming from a wounded theme of consciousness. Your true Self is perfect loving awareness. The greatness of your potential is pure innocence, stainless, and invincible joy. You are innately accepted, unconditionally loved, whole, and complete—despite what you've been through or what the external world is telling you. You are infinitely guided, supported, and provided for by your Creator. You have access to infinite possibilities right now. Your very existence is proof of how loved and cherished you are—even if you can't see it yet.

The question is, do you believe this? We invite you to read the next few lines out loud and honestly examine how you feel. We recommend pausing between each line so you can become aware of the sensations in your body in connection with each affirmation. Self-honesty is the first step in revealing your current anatomy of consciousness.

I am pure.

I am innocent.

I am already worthy.

I forgive myself and others.

I am wanted and needed.

I am seen.

I am free from my past.

I have no regrets.

I face my fears with courage.

I expect the best case scenario.

I have everything I need.

I am fully satisfied in my life.

I easily celebrate the success of others.

I have no enemies.

I am honest.

I go with the flow.

I trust I will always be okay.

I am unique and gifted.

I am talented.

I am inspired and inspiring.

I am a success. My life is a success.

I see only opportunities.

My life has extraordinary meaning.

My future is positive and bright.

Everything is working out for my benefit.

I am brilliant.

I have access to genius ideas.

I am intelligent.

I am at peace in every moment.

I am completely loved.

I see the goodness in everyone and everything.

I see Divine Love all around.

What do you think about all this? Pay special attention to any of the affirmations that made you cringe or squirm with discomfort or avoidance. Notice what the mind has to say. Perhaps something to the effect of, "This is stupid. You don't know *me*. This is just *too* much." Or perhaps it attempts to rush through and overlook the statements and not take them too seriously, "Okay, I get it, let's skip the next few lines. How long is this going to go on for? Yeah, yeah, love myself." All an attempt to run away and avoid looking at what is really getting triggered.

> *"You will never be free until you free yourself from the prison of your own false thoughts."*
> *- Philip Arnold*

This is our first demonstration of what your mind is doing to you when it is exposed to anything outside of your current spectrum of consciousness. The mind has created an identity for you that is unknowingly attached to suffering and limitation. This shadow identity doesn't want to let go of control and the familiarity of playing small because *it* is afraid of trusting in the goodness of life and *losing* its happiness. It is unable to truly accept goodness because it thinks that love and happiness are things that can be acquired, lost, or stolen depending on other people and circumstances. Yet the truth is, feeling happy, loving ourselves, and believing in the goodness of life are all *internal commitments* unrelated to the ever-changing, outer world. We are the only ones who are in control of how we experience our lives—we are that powerful.

The mind's defense against these optimistic affirmations is proof of the limitations it is putting on you and your experience of reality *right now.* In order to liberate yourself from the limitations of your mind, you must release and replace the **root program beliefs** which are preventing you from experiencing the love, peace, happiness, and freedom you are seeking. Anything and everything that is of the *not-Self* must go in order for you to break free. It is this inner shedding and letting go process which makes practicing *The Inner Work* uncomfortable at times. How tightly you cling to your old self-image will determine the difficulty of the process. You must have the courage to look at your shadows with honesty and take accountability. You must have the willingness to let go of rationalizing wounded behaviors and thought patterns. You might find that letting go is harder than you think because of your conditioning *to get, do, defend, prove, or blame.* Yet, the process of actualizing happiness has always been *an acceptance, surrender,* and *humble allowance.*

> *"We must be willing to let go of the life we planned,*
> *so as to have the life that is waiting for us."*
> *- Joseph Campbell*

Accepting More for Yourself

There are no boundaries to your happiness, divine abilities, and expressions of gratitude—if you only *surrender* resistance to accepting this truth. No one has more access to happiness, divine creativity, or greatness than you do. We all share in equal access to infinite joy, fulfillment, and peace. There is nothing actually to change, fix, or do "out there" in the world in order to actualize your happiness. The real solutions are all within you; you only need to *allow* them to come to you. You are the one in control of how much you resist or how much you receive—nothing else needs to change but yourself. You can do it!

When we resist our lives, we create greater separation from the truth of who we really are. The more separate we feel from our true Self of love and joy, the more powerless we feel, and the more powerless we feel, the more we suffer. We are inviting you to demonstrate your love for yourself by waking up to your own power. Accept that no one and no thing outside of yourself can ever steal your peace or your joy ever again. It's not about what has happened to you; it is how you decide to *respond* that determines the quality of your life. This is *your* life, and only you are in control of how it is experienced. Although it may be uncomfortable at first, the truth will empower you and set you free.

> *"The world we live in is the world we choose to live in,*
> *whether consciously or unconsciously.*
> *If we choose bliss, that's what we get.*
> *If we choose misery. We get that too."*
> - Tony Robbins

Exploring Our Resistance

Maybe your mind is thinking, "But my story is worse, or different, or this doesn't apply to me because..." Fill in the blank with your mind's favorite rationalization as to why you can't be happy and free *right now*, and you will see your own resistance clearly. That person, that situation, that past event, or future worry—whatever your story is, your *attachment to it* is the very thing blocking you from the true freedom and lasting happiness you are seeking.

> *"The first spiritual trap is to perceive your happiness*
> *as outside of yourself."*
> *- Dr. David R. Hawkins*

The good news is the rationalizations you are experiencing are just stories your mind is telling you. This means they are not intrinsically or objectively true—they are just *one* opinion and perspective out of infinite possibilities. We can always choose to see our past or current situations from a different perspective, and in so doing, everything about it changes. For example, we can see our setbacks as signs of our own weakness and inability, or we can see them optimistically as signs of growth, change, and evolution. It's not the setback itself that determines our experience of it, but our *perspective and response*.

As we continue along this journey together, you will begin to see that the mind's insistence on blaming things outside of itself is something that we all innocently inherited as part of being human. Have compassion for yourself as you explore your own resistances to being truly happy, and just know *your resistances do not define you.* They are something you are experiencing, but they are *not* who you are. Doing *The Inner Work* means your shadows and unhealed wounds will be revealed to you in order to be understood, accepted, and finally released and transcended. However, it is important to point out that your shadows will continue to evolve as you do. So you must always maintain humility and vigilance of any possible new blindspots as you progress. Every stage of human evolution has its own obstacles and temptations to be aware of. Therefore, *The Inner Work* is a contemplative lifestyle approach, not something to attain or a destination to arrive at.

Knowing the tenacity of the mind, you must be kind to yourself in order to fully heal any wounds you uncover. The best way to find compassion is to see that your experiences are impersonal and not actually *about you*, but just what you are *experiencing*. Do not confuse the limiting, internal dialogue inside your mind as the ultimate reality. One of our favorite sanskrit mantras to repeat is "neti, neti"—meaning "not-this." I am *not* my past. I am *not* my trauma. I am *not* this fear. I am *not* this thought. I am *not* this guilt. I am *not* this doubt. I am *not* this story.

In order to be reborn as your *true Self*, which is free from rationalizations and excuses, and to accept the infinite peace we speak of, you must release attachment to the shadow identity and resistances your mind has constructed over your lifetime. This may be difficult to do at first because an untamed mind will fight to reinforce its past programming. This defensiveness is not personal, just how the mind works. Wounded themes of consciousness like rejection, judgment, overwhelm, loss, distrust, inadequacy, violation, and insecurity become so familiar to us that the mind strives to defend its belief systems through an incessant **internal**

dialogue. This constant inner dialogue of thoughts will automatically reinforce, support, and seek validation for its perspectives. Unless we become aware of what is actually taking place, we will never be able to move on from it. Know that uprooting these mental narratives would mean the death of an identity the mind has worked so hard to formulate, and so we must have compassion during this revealing process. We all have accumulated rationalizations as to why we can't possibly be so loved, accepted, happy, and free *as we are*. The mind says things like,

"Don't embarrass yourself."
"You're not good enough."
"You'll just fail."
"What will they think about you?"

The mind tells us we can only be happy when other people or our circumstances change.

"If he would just ask me to marry him."
"If she would just stop nagging me."
"If I had more money."
"If I paid off my debt."
"If I moved."

The internal dialogue even tries to convince us that we need to struggle and fight for our deserved happiness.

"It's a cold, tough world out there."

"Better be the best if I want to succeed"

"There's not enough for everyone—better earn it."

"They are my competition."

These mental narratives of lack and limitation keep us from ever stepping outside of our conditioned spectrum of consciousness and experiencing something new and inspiring. Something so radical and extraordinary. Not because it is "special" in any particular way, but only radical because so few people *accept* it for themselves. All have equal access to happiness and greatness. If experiencing true love, lasting joy, and inner peace are rare, it is only because so few have the courage to put down their suffering and have faith in the goodness of life. Commitment is key. Notice that even when we're right on the cusp of becoming a higher version of our potential—the boundaries within the mind keep us in check by convincing us that we can't do it, it won't work, we'll look dumb, or it just wasn't meant for us.

"This probably won't work."

"I waited too long."

"What if I can't do it?"

"This is just the way things are. I'm fine with it. I should just stop trying."

We start to believe that we aren't one of the lucky, special people who get the opportunity of being so happy and carefree.

"Must be nice to be them."

"They are just rich."

"If I had their life, I'd be happy too."
We then attribute blame to our conditions, circumstances, and even the world for this plight.

"This system is so corrupt."
"The world is unfair."
"Life is stressful and hard."
"My situation is different. This doesn't apply to me. I can't change."

The most important realization of *The Inner Work* is that **the source of our dissatisfaction is the mind's internal dialogue, *not* the subject of its complaints.** Change is terrifying to the untamed mind. Even when exposed to true happiness through witnessing it in others, it will reject it outright through denial or projection. Most minds are actually very suspicious of someone emulating genuine innocence, unconditional love, and inner peace. Seeing someone else shine their light unapologetically can really trigger an insecure mind.

"They are so fake."
"They are so naive."
"They don't know what it's like to struggle."
"They just haven't had enough life experience yet. They'll see."

So although it is happiness and freedom you are seeking, it is crucial to recognize that even while you are yearning to elevate yourself, there is still a huge part of you, ***an ego***, *shadow identity* *stuck in a wounded theme of consciousness* that actually does not want you to succeed in awakening.

> *The only enemy to ever exist is an eternal one.*
> *It is hiding in the very last place you'd ever look.*
> *Within yourself.*

Our Collective Inheritance

Whether we are conscious of it or not, we all inherited limiting beliefs, thoughts, and programming that are counterproductive to our well-being and bring suffering. Over a long enough period of exposure, these beliefs become so familiar to us that they then formulate a limited identity within us. Whether this wounding came directly through parents, teachers, religious figures, friends, or indirectly through the influences of society—we all got it. These inherited limiting programs of belief are *not* personal, just part of being born a human. However, the most empowering view we can take on our suffering is that it may actually be playing a perfect role in our hero's journey of awakening.

> *"The universe doesn't make mistakes."*
> *- Chris Prentiss*

When seen from the highest perspective, our struggles are actually our greatest teachers, for they reveal to us personal opportunities for expansion. For example, "hitting bottom" may have been exactly what was needed in order to finally let go, have a change of heart, or see the bigger picture. Like sandpaper to wood, our challenges can soften the soul if we allow them. We mustn't run from the discomfort of life's lows but instead have the courage to lean into them with humility and curiosity. In every painful or challenging experience, we can benefit from asking ourselves, "What can I learn from this? What character quality can I develop from this? What do I need to let go of? What part am I playing in this? Where am I limiting my own joy and peace? Where am I getting stuck? Where can I expand?"

It is only by facing our resistances with self-honesty and accountability that we can experience the empowerment and happiness that is waiting for us on the other side. See your discomfort as the doorway to freedom. Have the bravery and courage to see all obstacles only as temporary moments of realignment—*always* working out in your favor.

> *"Your trials did not come to punish you, but to awaken you."*
> *- Paramahansa Yogananda*

The desire to hide, deny, or reject our insecurities, pain, anger, or sadness ultimately only hurts us further. When repressed and buried, our emotions will slowly poison us from within. For, every denial and rejection of our emotions is only a rejection of our Self. If we resist the existence of our shadows, they will only continue to thrive through our denial and fear of them. To feel is to heal.

The Inner Work process is an invitation to allow emotions, understand them with compassion, and finally release those that are not serving us. Nothing we feel could ever be *wrong*. We are all innocent, learning and becoming. Everything we go through is actually playing a perfect part in our own hero's journey of enlightenment. All seeming "mistakes" are only an innocent discovery of who we are *not*. Thus leading us one step closer to the truth of who we *are*.

The mind is naive and impressionable and therefore subject to massive error. We mustn't identify with the mind's perceived mistakes but rather seek to understand ourselves and others with compassion. By courageously acknowledging our vulnerabilities, we are on our way to healing them. Accepting ourselves as we are right now is the initial part of *The Inner Work* process.

> *"Your problem is*
> *you're too busy holding onto your unworthiness."*
> *- Ram Dass*

The Human Potential

Due to our unique ability to make conscious choices and exercise a **spiritual will**, humans are actually capable of experiencing dramatically different levels and rates of evolution, i.e., themes of consciousness. True freedom and lasting happiness are an example of a degree of evolution in human consciousness. Just as themes such as rejection, inadequacy, accountability, and understanding are as well. Each season of the human experience has differing inner obstacles, shadows, and attachments to overcome in order to allow a grander paradigm and view of life to come forth—continuously becoming more loving and free as we spiritually mature. Thus, the next stage of human evolution is not a physical adaptation but an evolution of consciousness—an internal shift that can only be brought about through the inner choice of peace, happiness, and love.

"Self-discipline is making the higher choice, again and again."
- Ellen Grace O'Brian

As each individual makes the higher choice to heal the wounded themes of consciousness, humanity as a whole will gradually adapt to new levels of maturity—eventually leading to inner-liberation for all. Therefore, every individual is important, needed, and a necessary part of the greater whole. Everyone must do their own *Inner Work*—no one can do it for us. We all share in the collective human karma or destiny. Every thought and action of the individual contributes to the collective consciousness and, in fact, all the universe—*there is no actual separation.*

You are a crucial part of a greater whole, deciding to be free from the inner shackles of limitation. Deciding to choose love, happiness, and the peace of remembering *who you truly are*. And while the effect of your choices will have immense benefits for you personally, the world will benefit a thousandfold. For every time we heal a personal limitation and trauma within ourselves, we are healing it within the collective as well by holding the door open for others to join us by following our example. Every advance in consciousness of the individual uplifts the rest of us with it like an ocean tide rising. There could be no greater contribution to humanity than doing your own *Inner Work*.

"Your own Self-realization is the greatest service
you can render the world."
- Ramana Maharshi

Consider this a formal invitation to finally experience the full joy and awe of Creation, to accept a life filled with purpose and meaning. It's all around you, waiting for you to simply recognize it. It is *right here, right now*. Have confidence in the love and support of your inner Self. Trust your true Self will come forth and is always with you. You will know the Truth by its essence of innocent joy. The energies of happiness, empowerment, compassion, kindness, trust in goodness, faith, peace, humility, satisfaction, fearlessness, and most importantly, gratitude are all some of the most powerful hallmarks of your true Self. Pay attention to the daily moments you embody these energies. Those will be the moments that you are living up to your full potential and living in your purpose. Those are the moments that you are *being* the love and happiness you've always desired, rather than trying to obtain, project, or earn it. Realize that all the joy of life is *within you already,* and you are destined to succeed, or else you wouldn't be *here, now.*

"Happiness is when what you think, what you say,
and what you do, are in harmony."
- Mahatma Ghandi

Chapter 3

The Human Plight

"There is pleasure and there is bliss.
Forego the first, to possess the second."
- Siddartha Guatama Buddha

We all have a deep yearning within our hearts to be happy. And we have amazing fantasies of how we wish to express that happiness, whether through travel, romance, or arriving at a milestone life goal. If you think about it long enough, you will realize there is definitely *somewhere* you would like to get. Some are seeking to meet the person they will marry so they can finally settle down, have children, and be happy within a secure partnership. For others, they won't allow themselves to feel freedom until they finish paying off their debt. And for many, they are anticipating retirement so they can finally have the time to relax and enjoy life.

Unfortunately, most of the time, these fantasies become a grand way of projecting our happiness outside of ourselves as something that we have to "get to," thus setting us up to suffer in the meantime. Yet, it isn't the dreams themselves that are the problem. Life is meant to be an adventure of possibility and fun—our visions and inspirations are gifts to explore. The origin of the problem is in the belief that life will *only* be better *when...*

The Truth of This Moment

The truth is that things can actually be better right now if you allow them to, even while you are still in the process of *becoming*. You don't have to wait until tomorrow or until some big event transpires to live your dream life and to feel your best. You actually already are living your dream life and already have everything you need to be happy. You only need to wake up from the nightmare of your *not-self* to see it. It is your birthright to be infinitely peaceful, joyful, and free in every new moment. But if this is the truth, why don't you feel this way all of the time?

Besides the fantasies about a future or past that is much better than this one, our mind will often deny us happiness in small doses subconsciously each and every day.

By holding onto past trauma, we deny ourselves healing.

By feeling self-conscious, we deny our own self-worth.

By finding fault in other people's actions, we deny ourselves compassion.

By feeling hopeless, we deny ourselves faith.

By collecting excuses, we deny ourselves our own power.

By clinging to our losses, we miss out on the miracles happening now.

By feeling skeptical, stressed, worried, paranoid, or anxious, we deny ourselves contentment and trust.

By feeling envious of the others, we deny ourselves abundance.

By waiting for the weekend to come, we deny ourselves presence and gratitude.

By becoming offended or defensive, we deny ourselves peace.

By holding a grudge, seeking revenge, or gossiping about other people, we deny ourselves security.

By seeking attention and validation, we deny ourselves completeness.

By operating on autopilot, we deny ourselves inspiration.

By reacting to situations unconsciously, we deny ourselves discernment.

By closing our hearts, we deny ourselves love.

If you are truly honest and compassionate with yourself, you can begin to see your own habits in some of these examples and begin to recognize where you may be denying yourself the very things you desire. Whichever aspects of your life you are not allowing yourself to experience: joy, peace, patience, compassion, love, gratitude, faith, or forgiveness, etc.—that is where your *Inner Work* lies. Not because you need to be a better person, follow a set of commandments, or adhere to some sort of moral code, but simply because it *feels* better to choose better. And if you want to live a life of true freedom and lasting happiness, choosing better starts within.

"It is better to conquer yourself than to win a thousand battles."
- Siddartha Guatama Buddha

Attachment to Our Wounds

This is the plight of humanity. We've been unknowingly lost in dissatisfaction and powerlessness through the attachment to wounded themes of consciousness. Themes which perpetuate themselves through our inner dialogue, perspectives, and beliefs—eventually becoming our overall experience of reality.

The projecting of our happiness outside of ourselves.

The resistance to what *is*.

The mindless chatter of our mind which judges everything and everyone.

The clinging to the past and obsession with the future.

The fear of the unknown.

The expectations which cause us to feel entitled and ungrateful.

All of these programmed limitations were taught and modeled to us by others who were innocently taught the same. As you do *The Inner Work,* you will learn how to heal and break free from the wounded themes of consciousness which prevent you from living your best life and instead receive a system upgrade. One of your *own choosing*, perhaps for the first time in your life.

We know this can be a hard pill to swallow at first, but lean into the discomfort, for your freedom is just beyond the boundaries of your mind's limiting confines. Have compassion and patience with yourself in your awakening process. We all have *Inner Work* to do. None of these limiting beliefs are actually who we are, and we all fall trap to them from time to time. It is just part of being human.

> *"Yoga (true freedom)*
> *is the resolution of the agitations of the mind."*
> *- The Yoga Sutras of Patanjali 1:2*

The Ego Persona's Formation

The first question to ask with all this new information is, "If the mind's programs I am running on are not who I am, then who am I really, and why do I have these programs at all?"

Imagine yourself as a child, maybe at five years old. At this age, nothing seems to bother you or stick to you for very long. You are happy, free, innocent, and present with each new adventure. Life is one big playground for you, and every day is a brand new opportunity to be in love, surprised, and inspired. So what happened to this innocent child of bliss?

As we grew older, we were encouraged to identify ourselves as separate from the world around us and form an identity or ego persona. With learning our name, which toys were ours, and which toys were theirs, the mind developed **mineness mentality**. With *mineness mentality,* we lost our sense of surprise and wonder and instead developed expectations and an urge to control the world around us. We started to expect our conditions to please us, because well, everything is *mine*. We then created our identity by means of accumulation. Belongings, appearances, achievements, friends, experiences, and even traumas became "mine" and who we thought we were. Our egos became master collectors in a sense. And because we confused who we were with a world entirely outside of ourselves, our identity was threatened every time life didn't go the way we wanted it to.

To deal with such uncertainties, our ego persona created mental programs in order to protect and defend itself. If it can't control others or the outside world, it assumes control over us in the form of thoughts and emotions that it believes will keep us safe. All expectations, judgments, and opinions about our lives and others are essentially the ego-mind attempting to convince itself that *it* is in control of a world it feels threatened by. Not knowing any better, we have spent our entire lives listening to the frightened voice inside our heads believing it was us. This is where all limiting beliefs, thoughts, and emotions begin.

> *"As long as you make an identity for yourself out of pain,*
> *you cannot be free of it."*
> *- Eckhart Tolle*

Imagine yourself again, that same innocent five-year-old. Your parents get into a fight, and it makes you feel something new—fear and doubt of love and goodness. You instinctually find that by covering yourself with a blanket, you feel safe and protected. So you start to wear this blanket as a costume to hide from the chaos. You go to school and your classmates taunt you just for being yourself. You feel ashamed and embarrassed. You decide one blanket isn't enough protection, so you add a second one to cover yourself up even more. If you didn't physically do this as a child, we can guarantee you did it metaphorically.

As you get older, you fall in love, but the person you open your heart to shuts you down. So you add another layer of protection over yourself. Your parents get divorced; you add another layer.

People let you down; you add a layer. Your big plans don't pan out; you add another layer.

Anytime you are unable to control your circumstances or the people around you, you are reminded of how powerless you seem to be, and so you protect yourself with yet another layer. Because of *mineness mentality,* your mind innocently collected these experiences as a part of your identity and has worn them all your life. After all, from your ego's vantage point, all of it is *mine*, and therefore *about me*—all my experiences must define *me*.

As time goes on, the free, happy, innocent child of bliss becomes buried deep underneath the layers of fear for so many years that even you forget your true identity. You've been wearing the protective layers for so long that you completely overlooked the fact that you could just take them all off at any point. Luckily, underneath the layers of past experiences you have dressed yourself in, you still remain the innocent and happy child. No matter how traumatic life has been, you are still innocent and free, beautiful and perfect, wanted and loved, seen and recognized—*just as you are*. And with a little decluttering of the mind's layers, the innocent child of bliss can finally be revealed once again.

> *"To enter the Kingdom of Heaven,*
> *become like a child again."*
> *- Holy Bible, Matthew 18:3*

Your Awesome Existence

The *true you* in yoga terminology is satchitananda. Existence, consciousness, bliss. In other words, *purity of awareness—perfect innocence, stainless.* But the layers of experience you carry have created a biased lens from which you are now seeing the world, i.e., a wounded theme of consciousness. This biased lens forms negative perspectives about life based on traumas of your past. And because you have identified with this limiting ego accumulation for so long, you innocently forgot the radical awesomeness of your very existence in the *present.*

Let's take a moment to acknowledge and celebrate the fact that you *exist*—right now. Magically somehow, in this vast universe, here you are, with no recollection of how you got here, living on a planet that is filled with infinite experiences to be enjoyed. It's unfathomable and mystical when you really step back and examine your existence. Yet, you exist *effortlessly and unasked.* Without fully understanding how or why, here you are! On top of this mysterious existence, out of infinite other possibilities for what life could have been—you are a human. And not just any human, you are *you!*

Think for a moment about what it means to be alive. We don't even have to try to make our heart beat for us or force our lungs to breathe. We have no idea the magnitude of the trillions of cells that carry out their functions for us to stay alive moment to moment. Our organs just work. The body just heals itself. It all carries on intelligently and effortlessly. It is overwhelming when we stop to consider what is actually taking place. The magnitude of this perfect moment is almost too much for us to bear if we truly allow ourselves to contemplate the mystery and glory of Creation. But yet, here we are. In it, *right now*—eternity.

However, most of us go about our lives completely unaware of the magic of existence all around us. This lack of awareness surrounding the *absolute gift of life* is another symptom of *mineness* and the entitlement it propagates. Mineness complains of boredom and rejects gratitude. It takes its life for granted becoming a victim—feeling powerless in "*my life*." Or it becomes arrogant and judgmental—"Everyone else is ruining *my life*." Mineness mentality is the equivalent to the tantrum of the two-year-old and can last a lifetime disguised in various forms. It is due to these limiting perceptions that we endure so much pain and suffering. Surrender of our existence to something Higher than ourselves is the only remedy to pull us out of our ego's "mineness delusions." Have courage to see the *gift* of your life and be forever grateful.

"Just as sun and moon cannot be reflected in muddy water,
so the Almighty cannot be reflected in a heart
that is muddled by the ideas of 'I and my.'"
- Ramakrishna

Contemplating the awesomeness of the universe and our very existence is a quick way to remember that none of this is actually ours, and nothing is owed to us. Ideal conditions are not owed to us. Creation is not owed to us. Our ego did not create all of existence. Our ego does not keep the body alive. *Something grander* is doing that *for* us—our ego just takes the credit.

"In reality, everything is actually happening of its own.
One's life is a continuous gift, and its continuity from moment to
moment is sustained by God, not by the ego."
- Dr. David R. Hawkins

Therefore, our ego's greatest mistake is to claim to be its own source of existence—oblivious of how it even came to be in the first place. It suppresses the truth of its need for humility and gratitude by instead believing itself to be its own God—thus capable of judgment of self and others, desire for control, and entitlement. This can either be subtle such as impatience (other people are taking *my* time), or as extreme and grandiose as kings, emperors, and pharaohs claiming to be gods demanding worship.

Even if you do see yourself as someone who believes in a Higher Power, look deeper into your suffering, and you may find the ego's God-complex hiding in subtle behaviors you may be unaware of. For example, do you ever have impatience in traffic and feel others are in *your* way? Do you ever feel like family members should clean up better so *you* don't have to? How about feeling like people are interrupting you and taking *your* time? Or that life *should* be different—according to *your* opinion?

The belief that anything *should be* how the ego wants it to be is its God-complex—no matter how trivial the topic. All of us face this ego mentality on some level until we do *The Inner Work* to acknowledge, understand, and surrender it. In reality, everything *just is what it is*. Every waking moment of life is a gift. A gift that is constantly being sustained and guided by a Divine Source beyond our ego's comprehension. The ego cannot truly know Divinity/God; only the heart and soul can. The ego cannot become enlightened, for enlightenment is the transcendence of the ego.

"Cleanse the mirror of your heart, and you will see God."
- Neem Karoli Baba

If you want to remember the truth of *who you really are* and begin to move beyond the limitations of the ego-mind, spend some time with nature. Contemplate the perfection of a flower, observe the magic and mystery of the night's stars, take a bite of a mango, deeply look into the eyes of another, observe the innocence of animals, hold someone you love as if it was the last time, look out over the vastness of an ocean, or just become aware of that fact that you are breathing.

All the melodramas that you believe make up your life, are only an illusion distracting you from the grander truth that you even get the opportunity to exist at all. Nature's wonder will reveal that you are no different than the life within the plants, the energy of the earth, sea, fire, and air, or the spirit of the animals. Your consciousness and gift of life is the same as all other life on this planet. All equally blessed to *be, experience, and exist at all*. All is equally Divine, perfect, and full of love—we just have to have the eyes to see it. Whether waiting in traffic, washing a dish, or getting interrupted, with the removal of *mineness* mentality, all moments can be experienced with the remembrance that life is a gift to be enjoyed and praised.

"This is the real secret of life—to be completely engaged in what you are doing in the here and now.
And instead of calling it work, realize it is play."
- Alan Watts

Rediscovering Your Innocence

The purpose of *The Inner Work* is to realize nothing is holding you back from pure joy in life except your own ego's inner resistances. Self-realization is the disassociation with the layers of disguise you have been wearing and re-association with your true Self of unconditional love.

It's the return to your childlike nature before you piled on the layers of mineness. An embodiment of pure surrender, pure trust, pure presence. Children and enlightened sages actually have a lot in common. Both are innocent, fearless, and present. The only difference between the child and the enlightened sage is naivety and wisdom.

As a child, you were *naively innocent*, and thus you allowed the outer world to dim your light. Now, as a practitioner of *The Inner Work*, you are *wisely innocent—choosing* to remain happy and innocent *despite* the struggles and challenges of life. This is your own testimony of the power of the Truth. Through your experiences, regardless of what has happened to you, here you are *still choosing to trust in love and the goodness of life*. That is what makes you truly courageous and powerful. That is what makes you wise.

You *Can* Do This

We know this discussion on the ego-mind can be a lot to face at first, and it's not meant to be insulting or overwhelming. It's meant to re-empower you and assist you in remembering the truth of who you really are. Push past the mind's initial discomfort and buckle up because this may be uncomfortable for a while, depending on how tightly the ego is clinging. Don't worry though, remembering the Truth will be worth it—guaranteed.

Look at it this way. You are *so* powerful that you *can* be happy, satisfied, and free *right now*, in the life you are currently living—despite your current circumstances. All you have to do is push past your ego's resistance, which is a monumental demonstration of your strength. Nothing external needs to change. You already have within you everything you need to transform your experience of life.

"All you see in your world is the outcome of your idea about it."
- Neale Donald Walsch

No matter what your mind is saying as to why your story is different or why you need your circumstances to change in order to be free and happy, disregard its excuses for now and keep reading. The truth is, we all have equal access to inner liberation, and it's entirely within our own control and power to access it. It's only a matter of choice, inner discipline, and exercising our spiritual will. No one can take this opportunity to choose from you. It's just a matter of accepting the truth of your innate empowerment and doing *The Inner Work* to stay there.

You are magnificent, perfect, whole, and complete. You are radiant, influential, full of love, and so important. Which is why it is imperative for you to realize the truth of who you really are. For all the suffering in the world comes from the *forgetting* of who we are.

This message was prepared and meant specifically for you. You are intended for so much more, and it is time to accept this: more happiness, more love, more gratitude, more peace, and more fulfillment and purpose. There is no limit on this thing called life. You have just begun to scratch the surface of your potential.

"Bondage is of the mind; freedom too is of the mind."
- Ramakrishna

Changing Your Focus

True happiness *is* lasting and ever-present. Not to be confused with the temporary hits of pleasure that come from external ego gratifications. We get tastes of pleasure when we are able to successfully manipulate conditions and people to meet our ego's expectations. It makes us feel like we are in control of our circumstances and this is satisfying to the ego's sense of *mineness*. *My* life, *my* circumstances, *my* desires met. While this may be temporarily satisfying, inevitably, circumstances will shift out of our control.

When this is revealed, the ego-mind becomes terrified of its lack of control. In order to cope with this fear of the unknown, it creates mental delusions through judgment, opinion, inner commentary, and constant evaluations of how life "should be" to mask its existential insecurity. In reality, the ego mind knows nothing but has the audacity to claim it "knows it all." When internalized, the ego judges itself harshly and cowers in fear at the challenges of life, and seeks to make us feel powerless and a victim. When projected externally, the ego's fear comes out through its desires to manipulate its conditions, circumstances, and other people through force.

Using force, however, will always leave it feeling defeated because life has a Divine Will of its own, which is far more powerful. We can only unlock the true fountain of freedom through **surrendering**. The ability to surrender to the Divine Will is actually the most powerful demonstration of our freedom. This is because surrendering requires us to have immense strength and inner discipline to consciously ignore the demands of a resilient, fearful ego. The ego is rooted in fear and lack and therefore cannot have faith and trust in something Higher than it. Whenever we consciously ignore the demands of the ego to either cower in fear and victimization or attack with aggression and force, we prove our liberation.

The one who is no longer servant to the demands of the ego-mind
is the only one who is truly free.

By challenging our ego's agenda, we take the focus off the external circumstances which it is resisting and instead focus on *the resistance itself.* Through this very conscious redirection of our focus away from our outer experience and into our inner one, we can access true freedom and lasting happiness. This might seem like wishful thinking since lasting happiness is not what you have been experiencing thus far in life. But that's only because we've collectively fallen asleep, become lost in a dream or nightmare that we can't seem to wake up from. Everyone you know probably believes their ego's thoughts, tries to control their circumstances, and has expectations of their external conditions and the people around them. And the fact that almost an entire species is living this way only makes it that much easier to go along with. It's like one massive con.

> *"The bigger the trick and older the trick,*
> *the easier it is to pull, based on two principles.*
> *They think it can't be that old, and it can't be that big,*
> *for so many people to have fallen for it."*
> *- "Jake Green" in the film Revolver*

Ignorance is still ignorance, no matter how many people are supporting it. This simple misunderstanding has mutated into an entire species lost in confusion of pain that was not necessarily intended and does not have to remain. The suffering of painful experiences in our lives and the lives of others around us have not been a reflection of who we are, but a reflection of who we are *not*.

The Con

Unknowingly we have allowed our outer circumstances, other people's actions, past traumas, and external gratifications or losses to determine how we feel inside, tell us who we are, and define us as a being. The ego's entire system of self-worth is externally dependent, thus leaving us vulnerable to disappointment and suffering. No matter how triumphant an ego may become in life, it ultimately must always face the inevitability of death and change. All external things will turn to dust. Hence Jesus' teaching,

"Store not your treasures upon that which moth and dust can
corrupt, but instead invest into that which is immortal
and of the Kingdom of Heaven."
- Holy Bible, Matthew 6:19 - 20

Just think about what happens to us when there are unexpected delays, the grocery bill is more than we anticipated, an obligation is sprung on us last minute, someone cancels on plans made weeks in advance, or perhaps our partner forgets to run an important errand we specifically asked for. The smallest of things can steal our joy. Sometimes for a moment or sometimes for an entire day. We may even keep a running tally of other people's actions to collect proof and validation of our ongoing disappointments. And those are just some of the common situations we experience in life. Now think about what happens to us when much larger, unforeseen, life-altering situations occur, like trauma, abuse, a death, global epidemics, or a natural disaster. Sometimes these events steal our happiness for weeks, months, or even years. This jaded mentality can seep into every corner of our lives.

On the other hand, circumstances can trigger glimpses of pleasure, like when someone compliments us, our bills are less than we expected, we get to leave work early, or our partner surprises us with a romantic gesture. We credit all of these experiences, good or bad, with the power to control our mood based on what is happening "out there." This is why we have spent our entire lives trying to control our circumstances.

The result of this externally focused perspective is that circumstance becomes the authority over our inner perception of life. This is ironic because all of life is actually an inner, subjective experience. This limited way of thinking will leave us forever riding a roller coaster of highs and lows, elations and sorrows. And while it is absolutely true that we are all interconnected and affected by each other and our environment, our perspectives and beliefs are *not* innately controlled by anything outside ourselves. We always have, and always will have, freedom of choice of how to *respond.* And it is the higher themes of consciousness which unlock our ability to transcend circumstances through powerful perspectives of love and optimism.

> *"Be happy for no reason, like a child.*
> *If you are happy for a reason, you're in trouble,*
> *because that reason can be taken from you."*
> *- Dr. Deepak Chopra*

Letting Go of Attachment to Circumstance

What if experiences and situations are just passing moments, like clouds moving through the sky? What if they are just what's *happening*, and you are just watching it all? What if everything will pass—the good and the bad? What if everything just *is what it is* beyond labeling and judging? What if none of it defines you?

It is impossible to own a moment, a situation, or experience, yet our ego can't help but cling and grasp. By becoming attached to our experiences as part of our identity, the ego causes suffering by blocking life's natural flow—like trying to swim upstream. Whether it's being stuck in the past or waiting for the future, we miss out on *now*. But it doesn't have to be this way. We can let go of our attachment to what is happening outside of ourselves and become free *within* just as the sky is unchanged by the clouds passing within it. The bliss of life *can* shine through us despite uncomfortable circumstances by practicing nonattachment and surrender.

> *"If you realize that all things change,*
> *there is nothing you will try to hold on to."*
> *- Lao Tzu*

Circumstance can only rule us so long as we declare it the ruling authority. It is actually *us* who hold the keys to happiness and contentment. It has always been us. By doing *The Inner Work,* we will inevitably uncover a deep satisfaction for life regardless of circumstance. A satisfaction we have had access to all along.

Self-Inquiry

The great philosopher Socrates urged humanity to examine one's life to the point of even suggesting it is not worth living otherwise. If we are to truly live, we must question the nature of our own thoughts and emotions.

Let's give this examination a try now. After reading these next few sentences, make an attempt to consciously quiet the inner chatter of your mind. Give yourself at least five minutes of complete inner silence. You can keep your eyes open, or you can close them. But see if you can allow yourself to sit in complete silence without the mind interrupting you with thinking. You can even set a timer. This exercise will help you understand the nature of your mind and serve as an asset in your *Inner Work* progression. Go ahead and try this now. Sit still and see if you can quiet the thoughts in your mind for five minutes.

How did it go? More than likely, this exercise was more challenging than anticipated. That is to be expected. Notice if judgment or frustration arises now that this exercise is over. That is still the ego-mind doing what it does best. Don't worry about it too much. Just take notes on what the mind did during the exercise and what it is doing now that the exercise is complete. You probably witnessed that the mind was impossible to control. And that is because it has been the controlling authority within you for far too long without you knowing it.

This is a great exercise, for it reveals the tenacity of the mind. How dominant it is within us, yet never questioned or even noticed. Although these thoughts are seemingly impossible to stop, you were however, *aware* that you were thinking, which changes everything. And if you are able to observe your own thoughts, who is actually doing the thinking? And who is it that is listening?

Who is the actual thinker of your thoughts? The immediate response might be, "Of course, it's *me*!" But if it is *you*, then why wouldn't you be able to just stop thinking, since after all, it's just you, right? How can a part of yourself not act according to your will?

Perhaps our mind is like any other cell or organ, carrying on its duty unconsciously, without our input needed, like our heart beating, or lungs breathing. The mind just *thinks*, unasked and without input on our part. This would make sense most of the time, except there are instances where we seem able to focus, concentrate, and direct our mind using our spiritual will. And it is this spiritual will that is the seat of intention and choice of our theme of consciousness.

So what is going on here? Perhaps the mind can function both involuntarily as well as willfully? *We've just never noticed the difference between the two.* Making this distinction is a colossal revelation in your hero's journey. Once fully ripened, this newfound awareness will awaken you to a paradigm of epic empowerment. For when the mind's behaviors are seen for what they really are, life will never be the same again.

> *"The mind is a wonderful servant but a terrible master."*
> *- Robin S. Sharman*

So what has the mind been up to when you're not paying attention? And how much of its incessant chatter has been affecting your perceptions, experience, and mood?

Have you ever really listened to your own thoughts? Some of it is coherent and focused, but most of the time, it seems to just be *happening*. The inner dialogue goes on constantly and attempts to narrate every single moment of your life, whether you want to hear it or not. It rambles on naming things, creating assumptions, and giving its opinion, moment after moment, all to provide itself with a false sense of security. All to make you believe that *it* is in control and that *it* is a real identity. The task at hand is to start to become aware of this constant dialogue that is happening inside your head and separate yourself from it. Become curious as to what each new moment might feel like if you could just turn the voice off.

"Why are those people looking at me? This is so embarrassing."
"I'm not good at this. I knew this would happen."

"She thinks she's so perfect, ugh, so annoying."

"That was so stupid. I shouldn't have done that."

"They should mow their yard."

"What's the point of trying?"

"This is so depressing."

"Why hasn't he called me back yet? Maybe he's busy, or maybe he doesn't like me?"

"I hope I don't get sick."

"Wow, she's so sexy."

"I never have any money."

"I can't wait to party this weekend."

"This is taking way too long. They should hurry up."

"Wow, people are stupid."

"I hate this."

"Screw them!"

"I probably impressed them. Of course, they're interested in me."

"I am definitely the most attractive person here."

"These people are so uneducated and closed-minded."

"I wonder how much money they make."

This voice narrates and edits its perception of reality all the time, constantly feeding us its biased perspective. A perspective that we internalize and attribute as coming from me. But go a little deeper. If it is *us,* then why can't we just stop it and control it? If we don't want to hear it, why won't it stop? Maybe the mind actually has an agenda of its own that is impersonal to us.

Liberation is Arising Right Now

Come deep into this moment with us now. Read these words and ask yourself, "Who is listening?" Really, who is listening to these words as you read them to yourself? And who is reading for that matter?

Is it the eyes? Perhaps the brain?…

The first place we might look to is the body. After all, we *are* these bodies, aren't we? But if we are the body, why is it that when our body changes with age or is altered through illness or accident we don't *feel* any less "me"? We always feel the same sense of "I." It is only the body that seems to change *around* us. With honest reflection, it seems what is more accurate is that we "have" a body, like a biological vehicle we're using to move through life, but it is not who we truly are.

So then who is reading, who is listening if not the body?

How about the voice of the mind that's narrating? "Isn't that *me* thinking? Aren't thoughts 'me' talking to myself?" But if we were our thoughts, how would we have an awareness *of* them? How could our mind be "me" if it is reading and processing the thoughts *for* something that is able to listen? Instead, there seems to be an unmoving awareness *behind* and *in-between* the thoughts that is *aware* of thoughts. By analogy, it is only the background of silence that allows for sound to be heard. So are we the sound or the silence, or both?

There's still something more. There's still another layer of our consciousness that we're overlooking. Who is even aware of all of this to begin with? Fundamentally, at our core, who is experiencing this human life? Who is processing the thoughts, "hearing" them, experiencing them? Who is experiencing this divine drama, taking in this reality we call life, *right now*?

To which we can't help but intuitively answer, *"I AM."*
Is that not the name of Divinity?

"Be still, and know that I AM."
- Holy Bible, Psalm 46:10

"I AM the Self seated in the hearts of all creatures. I AM the
beginning, the middle and the end of all beings."
- The Bhagavad Gita, Chapter 10, verse 20

"I AM a spark from the Infinite. I am not flesh and bones.
I AM light."
- Paramahansa Yogananda

PART II

Liberation from the Mind

Chapter 4

Meet Your Mind

"Don't believe everything you think."
- Allan Lokos

Up until this point, you have most likely approached life believing that the mind's thoughts are yours and that everything you think *is in fact—you*. A radical truth that we have not accepted as a species is:

We are not our thoughts.

As long as you confuse thoughts as who you are, you can never actually be free, for you will remain controlled by them. If your thoughts tell you stories fueled with anger and competition, you become angry and competitive. If they spin stories of fear and paranoia, you panic and have anxiety. If they grovel in shame and regret, you become depressed, and so on. Because we have never stopped to question our thoughts, we have, in turn, become obedient to them. So obedient that we even think we are the ones thinking them. We confuse thoughts *as* us. To question our thoughts would be to question our sense of reality and our sense of identity, maybe even our sanity. But you must have the courage to keep exploring. This chapter may be uncomfortable for the mind because we are going to be exposing its tactics of defense. See the resistance clearly. There is so much more to you than what you think.

This concept of watching your inner dialogue as an impersonal *observer* of it will reveal a theme of consciousness and cause an empowering shift within you. However, the ego-mind will do everything it can to convince you to stay subservient to it. This is to be expected, of course, because you are challenging the mind's sense of control and igniting the awakening process. All heroes' journeys must go through a shattering of their old reality in order to step into their authentic one.

Understand that the resistance of the mind is not out of some maniacal, sadistic behavior but purely out of ignorance and naivety. It is not an actual enemy, only an inheritance of being born human—same as having a heart, lungs, arms, or legs—it just is what it is. All references to the mind as an "enemy" throughout this book are simply to reveal that all perceptions of enemies are actually just the mind projected *as* that enemy. And so, it may be useful in the initial stages of our awakening process to see the *real* "enemy" clearly so as to stop playing into its games of projection and distraction.

From a higher perspective of love, the mind is like an innocent child and simply doesn't know any better, and it is ultimately doing what it believes will help it survive. It genuinely thinks it is doing what is best for you, even if it seems atrocious or horrific. It may be helpful to view the mind as an innocent machine or hardware going along with whatever inherited programs and software were installed into it. It literally does not have the ability to tell if a program is good or bad for it, just like a computer accepting a programmed virus without question. Thus something greater than the mind has to become aware of what is being programmed and accepted.

Commit now to becoming the watcher of your thoughts and utilize your observations to grow and change through your newfound awareness of the mind's incessant commentary. By paying attention to the quality of your inner dialogue, you will reveal your current theme of consciousness and your mind's root program beliefs associated with that theme. Remember, you are unconditionally loved and whole—even in the mind's confusion and wandering. You are not the theme of consciousness your mind has attached itself to. By having compassion for yourself and surrendering to the notion that *you are not your thoughts*, you will be able to make it through this revealing process. All of us inherited an ego-mind, and we are all in this together. On the other side of the ego's discomfort is eternal peace and freedom—have courage. Rise to the occasion. This is your moment.

"For the one who has conquered the mind,
the mind is the best of friends.
But for the one who has failed to do so,
the mind will be his greatest enemy."
- The Bhagavad Gita

How Did We Get Here?

Without guidance and awareness, we become entranced by the mind's thinking early in life. We even have entire education systems that reinforce the notion that the *mind is who we are,* and it should therefore be praised and developed as a personal achievement and point of pride. Yet, almost all of our thoughts are actually only reflections of past experiences and beliefs that have been modeled to us by those most impactful in our lives—parents, teachers, religions, friends, advertising, or society. In an effort to survive best, the mind seeks to quickly become in sync with the perspectives and themes of consciousness of the family and community. Thus we take on similar beliefs, thoughts, emotional behavior, and brain neuron development as those closest to us.

> *"Our social nature is such that we tend to meet*
> *the expectations of our elders."*
> *- Jean Liedloff*

Through community and influential figures in our lives, the mind absorbs and creates a mental narrative and a biological neuron blueprint—which we have been referring to as a theme of consciousness. Emotional habits, perspectives, beliefs, thoughts, degrees of success, abusive tendencies, worldview, religious perspectives, self-sabotaging behavior, quality of relationships, avoidances, attachments, neediness, insecurity, judgments, you name it, they all are a reflection of the different themes of consciousness we are occupying. Listening to the quality of your thoughts and noticing patterns and commonalities will reveal a theme of consciousness. For example, are your thoughts consistently pessimistic and doubtful, or perhaps optimistic and bold?

Through expectancy, we become entrained into certain themes of consciousness that then become our sense of reality—all without our conscious awareness. Even rebelling against our parents' or society's ways of thinking in order to prove our sovereignty is still yet another behavioral program inheritance. Without the original modeling, we would have nothing to rebel against in the first place. The question to be asking ourselves is *who would we be without any of these inheritances of programs*?

Who were you before you accumulated all your thoughts, programs, opinions, judgments, valuations, and attachments? Who were you before all your fear, doubt, and insecurity covered you? The true freedom and lasting happiness you are seeking can only be realized by breaking out of inherited programming and choosing to remember the truth for yourself.

> *"Until you make the unconscious conscious,*
> *it will direct your life, and you will call it fate."*
> *- Carl Jung*

Ego Accumulation—The Master Collector

Entrainment with different themes of consciousness is constantly happening to us with each new experience of life. The brain either strengthens or deconstructs neuron pathways with every repeated thought and emotion. The more a pathway is used, the stronger and more efficient it becomes, just like a muscle growing the more you work it. Shame, guilt, fear, anger, doubt, insecurity, impatience, judgment—all become strengthened and infused into our biological chemistry each time we choose to "go there." The habit of indulging in any particular emotion or thought pattern leads to that theme of consciousness becoming our automatic and effortless response to life.

Themes of consciousness are thus inherited, trained, conditioned, exercised, and reinforced until they gradually become subconscious and generate our sense of who we think we are. Things like skepticism, frustration, anxiety, or jealousy can become so hardwired into the brain that they become quite literally a *neurological reflex*. The brain can then become addicted to the chemicals released, called neurotransmitters, each time a neurological reflex is activated. The brain will even look for and find a reason or excuse to "go there" so that it can receive a *chemical hit* of the thought or emotion that it is so addicted to. The good news is, with each moment spent in states of gratitude, love, ease, and trust, the neuron connections for them get stronger as well, and the old pathways begin weakening. Thus through the same processes of expectancy and conscious awareness of which thoughts and emotions we are allowing ourselves to indulge in, we can make happiness a natural, habitual response to life—our original, pure state.

This is perfectly demonstrated in an old Cherokee folktale. Once, a long time ago, an elder sat by the fire and taught his grandson about life. He said to the boy, "There's a fight going on inside us all. A fight between two wolves. One is evil, angry, miserable, sad, resentful, prideful, and full of shame, guilt, and self-pity. The other is good. He is peaceful, happy, grateful, kind, benevolent, generous, truthful, optimistic, trusting, and compassionate."

The boy thought about life for a moment and asked, "Which one will win?"

To which the elder replied, "The one you feed."

The question to continually ask ourselves is, which wolf are we feeding?

After our mind has repeatedly been exposed to a specific way of thinking, it gets stuck in a self-perpetuating cycle. If a theme of consciousness is of a positive nature, this will be helpful, but the ones which bring suffering require uprooting. Inherited negative beliefs, perspectives, and thoughts that burrow into our subconscious continue to validate themselves through rationalizing support and resisting accountability and change. They keep us trapped in suffering through defending the very beliefs, thoughts, perspectives, and habits that make us feel powerless by placing blame outside of ourselves. Remember, none of this is your actual true Self; it is an example of how your limited ego-self maintains control. Behind these layers of limitation and skewed perception, you are still absolutely innocent and a marvelous creation of perfection.

Avoiding Discovery Through Blame

To avoid being discovered for what it is, the ego-mind projects our problems as coming from outside of us in order to keep us distracted from the real root of our suffering—the ego's attachment to a wounded theme of consciousness. This is how it hides in plain sight.

*"The greatest enemy will always hide
in the last place you would ever look."*
- Julius Caesar

By keeping us focused on the external issues of our life and blaming something outside of ourselves, we never think that something *within us* could be the possible source of all our problems. By believing that our anger, guilt, or sadness is created by other people or external situations, we help to strengthen that particular ego attachment and feed the neurochemical addiction. The mind is always thinking *something or someone else* is at fault, thus protecting itself from ever being discovered. However, the downside of this displacement is that in the process of defending itself, the mind accidentally makes us a victim by giving our power away to the external person, place, or circumstance it is blaming. Through committing to your *Inner Work*, you are peeling back the veil and seeing this human plight clearly.

Breaking the Cycle

Traumatized people tend to traumatize others. Those who blame tend to feel like victims which teaches others to be in blame with them. Those who are prideful tend to be hiding insecurity and try to make others feel insecure. Hurt people passing on hurt to others thus teaching them to repeat the behavior. And the innocent cycle of ignorance begetting ignorance goes on and on. The mind naively puts itself into a self-imposed prison of repeating cycles of suffering and confusion. Compassion for ourselves and others becomes natural when we see how this all works. While these cycles go on rippling throughout humanity, we don't even know there is a choice to be anything different than what we are—*until now*.

Luckily, the ego's past programs and self-sabotaging behaviors are just *one* perspective and view of life, not the *one and only*. There are infinite other perspectives, responses, emotions, and thoughts to choose from if we have the eyes to see them. It all starts with awareness. There is more to life than what we have previously thought, and we *can* radically change at any moment. There are entire worlds of possibility yet to be explored *within us*. Worlds of patience, satisfaction, fulfillment, peace, hope, love, stability, happiness, uninterrupted bliss, confidence, and faith regardless of what is going on in our lives.

Have courage to look beyond your current perspectives and beliefs. Continue to question your mind and why you think the way you do. Inquire as to who you truly are—whatever the cost may be. Your curiosity as to why you suffer is the key to set your Self free. Know that the discomfort of the ego is to be expected and is actually a sign you are onto something true. If it wasn't true, it wouldn't threaten the ego. Our ego's discomfort is the doorway to our liberation. Be willing to step into it. Lean into it even.

"The day you decide that you are more interested in being aware
of your thoughts than you are the thoughts themselves
- that is the day you will find your way out."
- Michael A. Singer

Waking Up

By becoming aware of the constant mental commentary about our lives, we wake up from the matrix of our own thoughts. We unplug ourselves from the neuron pathways and patterns of suffering that are automatically reacting for us. The beautiful thing about our brain is that it can adapt and change over time as we exercise our spiritual will to override our current programming. It is moldable and has what scientists call plasticity. But in order to fully heal these neuron pathways of suffering, we have to understand them and accept them with compassion and humility—only then can we move on.

Self-Analysis

Take a moment and reflect on some of your most common thought patterns, such as the most significant beliefs like your self-worth, spiritual view of self, or how you think life tends to go for you. Examples might be:

"No one loves me. Everyone rejects me. I shouldn't be this way. God can't possibly love me. I should know better. I am wrong. I deserve to be punished. I'm incapable. I'm a burden. No one wants to help me. I always lose. People always abandon me. I lose everything I love. People are out to get me. They want me to fail. Fear keeps me one step ahead. I never seem to have enough. I deserve more. God is withholding from me. Everyone is in my way. I expect to get what I want. I hate setbacks and waiting. I am the best, smartest, and most attractive. I know what is best. I am superior and others are inferior. God favors the *chosen ones*."

Or perhaps they are of a more positive nature:

"I am committed and dedicated to goodness. I can handle the responsibilities of life with integrity. God is just. There is enough for everyone. There is no hurry. Arguing doesn't change anything. The world does just fine without my opinions. I don't need to get involved. I am talented. I am always doing my best. I enjoy being a great service to others. Life is filled with opportunity for me. Everything is always working out for my benefit. My life is a glorious gift. I forgive others and can appreciate everyone's uniqueness. Knowledge is power. It is wise to be a loving person. It is rational to seek the betterment of self and others. I am loved and love others easily. I am always supported and guided. I am completely loved and sustained by faith. God loves me unconditionally."

Either version of the stories came from somewhere. Whether of a positive nature or a negative nature, they were *installed* into us through experience, modeling, trauma, or adopted out of defense or curiosity. Take a moment and acknowledge that almost everything about your mind's perspectives, beliefs, judgments, values, and desires were *inherited and modeled or developed as a coping mechanism*. Some were beneficial, and others were not. But nevertheless, you have to accept that had you been born into a different family, different time, different country, different religion, different gender, or just overall had different life experiences, your thoughts and beliefs would have been completely altered. So who are you without any of these inheritances? What innocent, pure soul is underneath and behind all these messages?

Whatever our inner narrative is, conscious of it or not, our mind will always find a way to rationalize why it is *right* and the *best* way for us. This is how it maintains boundaries of control and is what society typically refers to as someone who is "closed-minded." The mind can be incredibly tenacious and resilient. The untamed mind is obsessed with being "right," "making a point," or being "justified," even if it brings suffering or death. As an extreme, Adolf Hitler, for example, believed he was completely justified and "right" in his thoughts and actions even at the expense of millions of souls.

The mind is innately limited, biased, and naïve. We may think that just because we're adults, we all "should know better," but that just isn't the case. The mind does *not* know better, or else it would do better. Compassion is therefore crucial. In fact, the greater the aggression, pride, or selfishness, the greater compassion needed for the torment going on within the mind exhibiting such behavior. Like can only come from like—hate does not come from love, and love does not come from hate. Aggression and violence being expressed to others can only come from a mind that is aggressive and violent toward itself.

True power, security, and love don't hurt others and have no enemies, only ignorance and lack do. We are all projecting our current spectrum consciousness at any given moment. We're all trying our best with what we were given. Underneath it all, we are always innocent, no matter how grotesque and faulty the ego judges others or ourselves to be. Remember always that we are *beyond* this; we are *beyond* this human body and mind. Begin to not take it so personally but instead seek to understand with humility and compassion for the human condition.

The Mind as a Computer

From a more nonattached perspective, we can view the mind as an amazing machine or tool rather than an actual identity. The suffering in our life has come from believing the mind's stories are what define us as "*me*." When actually, just like the heart beating so that the body may continue on living, the mind only perceives, translates, and processes the external stimuli of life to help us best survive and make sense of our external world. The mind can't *know* anything in its own right though. The mind can only attempt to *know about* things. It is only a processor of information, just like a computer.

The mind's library is made up of a collection of descriptions, categories, and symbols. It can't possibly compute the infinite details within any given moment accurately and even has a hard time remembering where it put the car keys. It is completely incapable of grasping the grandness of its own existence, but yet still somehow tricks us into believing that it knows everything. Witness how it has an opinion on just about everything and everyone. Even on subjects it has never actually researched, it still will come up with something. It is all a grand vanity—it does secretly, at its core, believe itself to be a god after all.

On top of that, it is only capable of seeing things *a* way—not *all ways* and therefore lacks humility and acceptance of its limitations. Our true Self, which is beyond the mind, is the one who actually *knows* by virtue of being *All That Is*. At which point nothing needs to be said, thought, or proven, for it *just is*. Existence, or *beingness—complete presence in the moment,* is the nature of our true Self. Meanwhile the mind only describes life on the superficial level, never capable of grasping its full divine essence. We all *know* we exist, but it's not something we can necessarily explain or quantify, nor is it required. Ironically, our fullness of potential is when we are the most humble, present, and don't have anything to prove.

> *"What I know is that I know nothing."*
> *- Socrates*

Our Ego Character and the Play of Life

The ego-mind is the *source* of all our negativity and suffering, and yet we have innocently listened to it ramble on while it attempts to solve its self-created problems. The mind's agenda is to continue perpetuating its limited narratives so it can remain the center of its universe. Its constant thinking helps it feel in control. In a sense, humanity's interactions are just a giant projection of our collective psyche. The great psychiatrist, Carl Jung, referred to it as the collective unconscious, in which we all play out roles and archetypes of characters in conjunction with the whole.

> *"The collective unconscious*
> *contains the whole spiritual heritage of mankind's evolution*
> *born anew in the brain structure of every individual."*
> *- Carl Jung*

The mind subconsciously puts itself in dangerous or pressured situations so it can be the failure or hero, it wallows in suffering to be a martyr or pious, it sees life as hard and full of challenges in order to be a champion or a victim, and so on. All roles ultimately are imaginary and attachment to them has to be shed eventually if we are to know true peace.

Being in the World but not Attached to It

When we are living in our ego, it is like an actor getting consumed into their role so deeply they forget who they really are—unable to return to their original state of consciousness. We might become frustrated or bitter as to why life doesn't feel authentic, like something is missing or "off." Thus we search our entire lives trying to fill a void that is coming from thinking something needs to change "out there." Never thinking that what needs to change is actually "*in here.*"

True freedom and lasting happiness are found in the balance between effort and nonattachment to your roles. By giving your very best in all that you do and simultaneously letting go of the outcome or merit, you will be truly fulfilled and full of joy. Whatever you are called to do, know that you were born to play your perfect part in this grand symphony, and it can only be you to do it. No one else can be you. That is why this is *your* hero's journey—for it can *only* be you. You are the one. You are absolutely vital, wanted, and needed. Each one of us has a specific, meaningful part to play in this great theatre of the Divine. And yet, with that being said, do not take your role in life so seriously that you make living a burden.

"They are enlightened who join in this play knowing it as play,
for people suffer only because they take as serious
what the gods made for fun."
- Alan Watts

If we know the mind likes to play these characters, then we are *in the world but not of it*—not attached to the role as "me," but rather something we're just playing at. Something we're witnessing arise and come forth as an expression of life. Life is not serious but rather *play*—only the ego takes things seriously due to the attachment to *mineness*. We can let the ego make life all about *me* and *mine* and therefore suffer, or we can surrender to the mystery with humility and find gratitude in all things. Knowing always, "This too shall pass—the good and the bad."

"Renounce and enjoy."
- Mahatma Gandhi

Chapter 5

Anatomy of Thought &
the Beneficial Use of the Mind

"Everything is energy and that's all there is to it.
Match the frequency of what reality you want
and you cannot help but get that reality. It can be no other way.
This is not philosophy, this is physics."
- Albert Einstein

Before any thought comes into your mind, it can be imagined as first floating in an infinite ocean of potential, waiting to be expressed. The Divine Unmanifest—infinite potential—anything is possible. Then, just as a radio has the ability to tune into a variety of stations over the airwaves, your mind, in the same way, is simply an antenna *receiving* thoughts depending on which frequency, or theme of consciousness, you are tuned into. In quantum physics, this is referred to as the Heisenberg Uncertainty Principle, in which human consciousness affects physical reality and not the other way around.

Everything is Available

All discoveries, inventions, cures, and answers to societal issues are waiting to be manifested through our inspired thought and action. We actually need to prepare ourselves for *receiving* and *allowing* such genius ideas. They can't be forced or sought out, only *invited* to be *realized*. Thoughts are picked up from the infinite field of consciousness and are always gifts and never actually ego-generated. Beware of credit-seeking—only the ego wants credit.

> *"My brain is only a receiver, in the universe there is a core from which we obtain knowledge, strength, and inspiration."*
> *- Nikola Tesla*

The irony is that our western society has taught us that thinking is the only way to solve a problem—as if it is something that takes effort, strain, and deserves praise. But it is actually a *surrendered*, *receiving* attitude which is most effective for insight. And even then, it is not personal or coming from a *me*. True genius is *given* and accompanied by humility. Therefore it is wise to practice giving thanks for all beneficial thoughts and simply release all that bring suffering. Be unattached in both cases.

> *"Everything comes to us*
> *if we create the capacity to receive it."*
> *- Rabindranath Tagore*

The ego-mind can only think about and fantasize about things it has already been exposed to, like a database of memory and past programs. That's why we tend to say things such as, "my mind is spinning," or "my mind won't stop," because it goes in circles repeating thoughts from its past index library in an attempt to "figure things out" or just ramble when you're trying to go to sleep. When the mind is constantly active rehashing the past or projecting into the future, it is not able to be truly present and therefore receptive to genuine insight within the *now moment*—which is the only "time" inspiration could ever arise.

In order to receive a new thought, we must get silent and still. When we are able to create spaciousness in the mind, we then open ourselves up to receiving genuine inspiration. With practice and devotion, this surrendered presence of inspiration can eventually become our every waking moment. This has often been referred to as "flow state," in which the mind is silent, and inspiration flows unencumbered as we are deeply present and responding in the *now*. The body just knows what to do, and creativity and inspiration come forth effortlessly. We just *know*, beyond thoughts.

> *"The quieter you become, the more you can hear."*
> *- Ram Dass*

Silence isn't empty. It's full of answers. Everything you could ever desire to know is available to you. The mind fears silence because it believes that if it stops thinking, it might go insane, nothing will get done, or perhaps it will even die. And so, out of familiarity, the mind never stops thinking due to fear of the unknown of silence. Yet, in the silence of the mind, all continues on joyfully without need for commentary. We must be brave enough to find out for ourselves and trust we will just know what to do and say, everything will still get done, and life will carry on beautifully. In fact, we will go about our lives without fear, stress, or insecurity—all products of the ego-mind. Could you even imagine it? No more fear, no more worry, no more doubt? This is your potential and your destiny.

Paying Attention to the Station

Because thoughts are "downloaded" and given to the mind, it's important to become aware of which station, or theme of consciousness, you are tuned into. Do you find that you are often tuning into the station of frustration or anger? Are you impatient or dissatisfied? Are you always thinking about what is wrong or missing—what you *don't* have? Or are you embodying the theme of love and inner peace and thinking about all that is right, good, and aligned in your life?

If you are not consciously choosing a frequency, by default, you will either become the frequency of your environment or the frequency of a past program. Just as you would change the station of a radio to hear different music, you must change the theme of consciousness you are tuned into if you want to experience different thoughts and emotions. Through consciously exercising your spiritual will you can tune into a new station, and your mind will become the receiver for a new wave of thoughts. It is through your declaration and *invitation* for something new that inspiration flows. This is one of the ways the mind can work *for* you and be a tool of inspiration and intuition in this physical world.

"Put yourself in a positive frequency to think positive thoughts,
and you will change your life."
- Dr. Wayne Dyer

Viktor Frankl, a Holocaust survivor, and Austrian neurologist and psychiatrist taught that in every moment there is space between the situation and how you are going to respond. You can either react unconsciously—repeating a past behavior—or you can respond consciously in a new way. Your reaction or response *is* the frequency you are choosing to align yourself with in that moment. Emotional states of your energy are the most obvious indicators of which theme of consciousness, or frequency, you are aligned with. Thoughts are what songs are playing on that station. Therefore, thoughts are the mental commentary—perspectives, judgments, belief systems, past memories, future speculations—that accompany the emotional state and serve to validate and reinforce it. By understanding the relationship between thoughts and emotions we can use them as tools for greater self-awareness and take back our power to choose our destiny.

Don't let your ego choose the station anymore. The first step to reclaiming your power to consciously respond is to develop awareness.

Chapter 6

Presence & Awareness of the Observer

"Presence is a state of inner spaciousness."
- Eckhart Tolle

The practice of watching the mind and its impersonal, constant stream of chatter creates a sense of separation and dissociation from the commentary. Once we are able to step back from engaging in the thoughts, we discover a silent, unchanging awareness behind them that is simply observing without attachment. Because we are no longer on auto-pilot—believing and going along with the mind's stories without question—we are finally able to *choose* for ourselves which theme of consciousness we indulge in. Without awareness, we will just go along repeating our past cycles and keep blaming external circumstances.

Awareness catches the mind red-handed in its attempt to project its issues outside of itself and takes accountability. This is an achievement of epic proportions. It is like waking up and realizing we were in prison when ironically we thought we were free. While this may seem dismal at first, it's actually incredibly empowering. So long as we are unaware of our hypnotic imprisonment, we will happily go on being enslaved to our ego's biased perceptions of reality and the suffering they are causing us.

> *"People have no clue that they're in prison,*
> *they don't know that there is an ego,*
> *they don't know the distinction."*
> *- Leonard Jacobson*

From a place of awareness, you can see clearly what is playing out in your mind—and therefore be separate from it, see it as the computer and receiver that it is. With awareness, you can actually implement lasting change by having compassion for yourself, your previous beliefs, and then gently and simply letting it all go. Your true Self is not afraid, judgmental, worried, angry, revengeful, jealous, shameful, etc. these are all limiting thoughts of the ego—not *you*. Awareness allows you to pause and find the gap between any situation and your response to it. Thus, breaking the patterns of wounded themes of consciousness by finally choosing something different.

It is through awareness that we begin to do our *Inner Work*. We cannot heal something we are unaware of. With awareness, the ego-mind could be spinning in a storm of panic and fearful thoughts, but we can remain the calm eye of the storm, still and unmoved amongst it.

> *"In moments of chaos, let me bring peace."*
> *- Jonathan Lockwood Huie*

Presence

While awareness watches the mind's chatter, presence goes beyond it entirely and transcends all wounded themes of consciousness. Through watching the mind, we naturally become curious as to what life might feel like without all its noise—thus evoking our first encounter with Divine presence.

Presence lives without the ego's editing of reality and therefore experiences life radically *as it is*. Without indulging in the mind's perspectives and thoughts, we experience life in slow motion— taking in the richness of every detail free of judgment. It is the notion of switching focus from content to the context. We take in the wholeness of every moment. The sound of our fingers caressing fabric, the texture of the linen, the smell of the detergent, the sunlight dancing through the window, the cool air entering our nose, and the hum of the insects outside all come into focus at once, even in a seemingly mundane moment of lying on the couch. A simple moment such as this has the ability to bring us to tears in gratitude for life. All of which normally gets overlooked and ignored because our attention is completely distracted by the busyness of the mind. In a state of presence, it is as if all of life is transformed into an all-encompassing divine movie or magical dream.

Yoga, meditation, breathwork, and plant medicines are all wonderful tools for *temporarily* accessing presence, thus can help us preview higher themes of consciousness. However, these are only tools to awaken possibility. They are not the source of these euphoric states and can only temporarily subdue whatever wounded themes of consciousness we struggle with. To transform our state of consciousness and live in presence permanently, we have to do our *Inner Work* to heal and release our ego's attachment to wounded themes.

> *"Neither breathing nor physical yoga exercises are of any use*
> *until you have grasped the idea:*
> *'In reality I am nothing but a witness.*
> *Nothing can touch me from outside.'"*
> *- Vivekananda*

Practicing Presence

Gratitude to Evoke Presence

The most powerful attitude and outlook on life is *gratitude*. In the state of gratitude, there can be no suffering. There is no lack nor fear. There are no limitations nor enemies. Gratitude sees all with perfect trust and acceptance and takes in the glory of the moment through being present with *what is*. Presence can be reached at will if we decide to simply take moments throughout our day to shift our inner narrative to one of gratitude and humility. This is most easily done by dropping deeply into the current moment and taking in all the overlooked, beautiful details of life.

Meditation for Presence

Meditation is simply sitting with the intention of watching the mind. It is a great tool to develop acknowledgment of awareness and to access states of presence. In order to strengthen our ability to maintain awareness and presence, we simply practice the self-reflection exercise we did before. Gradually extending the time we can sit watching the mind and withdrawing attachment to it.

Instead of attaching to thoughts as *mine*, we observe them impersonally. "*A* thought of shame arising. *A* feeling of fear coming up." It all just *is*. Nothing to do, nothing to change, nothing to figure out. Just observe. We become the sky and stop identifying with the temporary, passing clouds in a sense.

> *"Thoughts are only discernible if they move in a field of non-thought. The background of the mind is therefore the silence of the field of consciousness itself."*
> *- Dr. David R. Hawkins*

The more you practice, even if it's five minutes a day, the more empowered you will remain. This can then evolve into constant mindfulness that stays with you throughout your day-to-day interactions. Formal meditation is useful, but in order to evolve our consciousness, we have to make the transition into a contemplative lifestyle in which awareness of our thoughts and emotions is continuous. By practicing *The Inner Work*, the door opens for true, lasting transformation. Even the smallest, mundane moments of life become ripe for a breakthrough, such as sitting in traffic revealing attachment to anger or pride and therefore providing an opportunity to surrender and transcend the ego's limitations.

Through awareness, we can consciously refrain from indulging in our habits of frustration and impatience and instead tap into presence—witnessing the beauty all around us. The sunset behind the mountains. The breeze through the window. The music playing on our radio. All of it comes into full focus as we realize that we even get the opportunity to drive a vehicle, exist on planet earth, in a human body, right here, right now. Thus remembering our epic existence and affirming all that is beautiful, supportive, and good in our lives that our ego is overlooking.

Implications

Reclaiming presence is monumental in its implications, for it drastically shifts our perspective regarding our own life and others. As we practice, we experience how incredibly difficult it is to stay present and how much we have working against us as humans. The mind's chatter is incessant, society's indoctrination is relentless, and the onslaught of over-stimulating distractions make it almost effortless to become consumed into sensations and thoughts. Seeing this, we can drop all self-judgment and accept ourselves and others on a level we never comprehended before.

Our thinking has been biologically inherited, programmed, and modeled and is running based on subconscious patterns without us knowing it. *We think it's us*. We didn't know the distinction; we didn't know there was a difference. Initially, this came from our primal, animal nature to survive but eventually morphed into a flawed, limited perspective of reality—and we did it collectively as a species. But in the same way, humanity will one day awaken through each individual committing to their own *Inner Work* and healing the wounded themes of consciousness.

Coming across this knowledge alone is a massive step in remembering who you truly are. For if you know where to find the root of your suffering, you can finally pull it out instead of trimming the leaves. For the first time, you are fully aware of how your ego is trying to use your life force and distract you in order to perpetuate old patterns of belief and suffering. All of which, until this point, was not consciously determined by you.

PART III

Liberation of Consciousness

Chapter 7
Overview of the Themes of Consciousness

"The awakening of consciousness
is the next evolutionary step for mankind."
- Eckhart Tolle

The last aspect of our human experience to discuss before we get into the practice of *The Inner Work* is the themes of consciousness and their influence in our lives. While the mind is constantly fluttering and uncontrollably chatting about one thing to the next, our themes of consciousness can be a more consistent and reliable place to work from if we learn to identify their patterns within our lives. Using awareness, we can reveal how absolutely every aspect of our lives is colored and influenced by the themes of consciousness.

The Themes of Consciousness

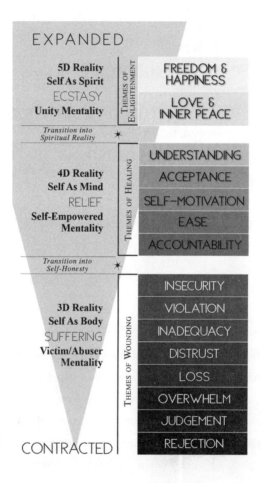

Lessons from Water

Dr. Masaru Emoto was able to visually demonstrate the variations of different themes of consciousness in his book, *The Hidden Messages in Water*. Dr. Emoto captured the effects that vibrational frequencies had on frozen water crystals using a powerful microscope with high-speed photography. He conducted experiments that consisted of exposing water to different positive and negative speech, positive and negative thoughts, various types of music, and even photographs. He then froze the samples of water to examine how the formation of crystals aesthetically changed. His experiments showed that water exposed to higher calibrating frequencies, such as love in the form of positive speech and pleasant music, generated uniquely beautiful, symmetrical crystals. Whereas the water exposed to negative frequencies, such as shame or anger, yielded unformed and asymmetrical crystals. The physical representation of each crystal formation is a perfect visual of how themes of consciousness manifest into the physical realm.

[Emoto, M. 2011. *The Hidden Messages in Water.*
New York: Atria Books.]

Similar to the crystals, a person occupying a wounded theme of consciousness, such as distrust, will create a life that looks and feels like distrust. They will experience thoughts of worry and doubt. Terror will surround them. They will experience feelings of paranoia and distrust. They will perceive enemies, whether physically or mentally. They will feel anxious around other people. Their choice of words will often be full of pessimism or panic. When they look at the world, they will see fearful concerns, instability, and jeopardy. Their body may manifest physical issues caused by chronic unresolved fears.

In the same way, a person whose theme of consciousness is calibrating in an enlightened frequency, such as love and inner peace, will, in turn, create a life that looks and feels like love and peace. They will experience thoughts that are compassionate and kind. Their bodies will usually radiate health and wellness. They will feel grateful for all the people and experiences in their life. Laughter and beauty will surround them. They will see the silver lining in every situation. Their choice of words will be full of intention and optimism. When they look at the world, they will see divine love and perfection.

Example Viewpoints from Each

Theme of Consciousness

To further demonstrate the varying themes of consciousness, let's look at how each theme might experience debt and credit.

From rejection, extreme debt may be seen as proof of our cursed existence and worthlessness. Suicide may seem like the only way out. In judgement, we may obsess on our debts as a demonstration of our stupidity and how wrong we are for having it, or project blame onto credit companies for how vile and wrong they are for "enslaving" us all. In overwhelm, our debt is completely paralyzing. We possibly give up on making payments as it seems pointless even to try. We feel there's no way out and accruing interest will just keep us trapped forever. In loss, we might dwell on how much we are losing everyday through interest. We might regret our purchases and overall feel our situations is sad and depressing.

From the perspective of distrust, we may look at our debt with paranoia and scare ourselves with worst case scenarios, "What if I'll never be able to pay this back? What if I lose everything?" In inadequacy, we may see debt as an opportunity to chase our pleasures and are excited to spend money we don't actually have yet so that we can get what we want now. In violation, we may view our debt with annoyance, frustration, or even rage at the accruement of interest—cursing aloud each time we receive an unexpected bill, which feels violating. Insecurity will either be overly obsessed with its credit score and its "smartest" and "best" use of credit, or it will use debt to inflate its appearances through expensive or "impressive" purchases, but in reality, be hiding incredible amounts of insecurity and debt accumulation.

In the theme of accountability, debt is finally seen with the integrity of honor. We commit to paying back our debts by courageously doing what must be done to repay, even if it takes a lifetime. In ease, debt is seen impartially and is what it is—we feel whatever happens, we'll be okay. Thus even if we have debt, it doesn't really affect our day-to-day life. In self-motivation, debt is seen as an amazing opportunity to launch business ventures, investments, and is seen as an ally in achieving our goals and ambitions. Acceptance sees credit and loans as a useful part of our lives. We don't care to rationalize or debate why the financial institutions are set up the way they are, but nevertheless use credit with responsibility and acceptance of our limits. From Understanding, credit and debt is seen as a fascinating creation of the financial world that, if used wisely, can actually benefit us if we know how to leverage it with cleverness. Thus we learn creative ways to make more money from credit and debt though things like investments, tax deductions, or interest working in our favor.

Finally, from the perspective of love and inner peace, credit is viewed with gratitude for the help we are being offered in our moments of need. We see that the Creator is giving us a gift for something that we need right now in order to advance our lives to another level of growth and evolution. We have faith that we will be provided a way to pay back the principal and interest with ease. All we are required to do is put forth our best effort—God will provide the "how." In peace and love, we believe everything is working out for our benefit and so use credit and debt wisely.

True freedom and lasting happiness represents the transcendence of the physical reality where nothing in the external world could ever affect our internal world. Thus everything is seen as a holographic projection of consciousness and is just to be experienced and not attached to. We wear any debt or positive credit like a loose garment, not letting it ever affect our internal state. Nothing of this world actually defines us. The world becomes a divine reality of Creation for us to enjoy with a heart of love and goodness. This is not to be confused with lack of integrity and recklessness, which would be reflective of the limiting themes —we are spiritually mature innocence embodied and have all the beneficial wisdom of the previous themes. Thus credit is used with ultimate intelligence and guidance.

This is just one example of how each theme has a very specific and unique perspective of reality and is why we see so much diversity amongst humanity. We all could be experiencing the exact same situation or circumstance, but based on our current theme of consciousness, we will interpret, and thus respond, completely different to it.

Our Habitual Themes

We call them *themes* of consciousness because the vibration you settle into will paint a consistent energetic pattern, or theme, throughout your life and will continue to show up whenever an opportunity presents itself. These themes will stay with you an entire lifetime unless you consciously address them. Just as good soil will bear good crops, your thoughts, words, feelings, desires, habits, and interests are intrinsically rooted in a theme of consciousness. Negatively charged themes will produce negatively charged thoughts, feelings, and actions, while positively charged themes will produce positively charged thoughts, feelings, and actions.

Within each theme of consciousness, root program beliefs will find validation, support, and expression through our repeated thoughts, feelings, and actions. This then creates neuro-programs that we begin operating on subconsciously—hence the term autopilot. All of this makes up our subjective experience of reality. If we are not aware of this process, we will naturally think the problems of our life are coming from "out there" when really it is all coming from our internal theme.

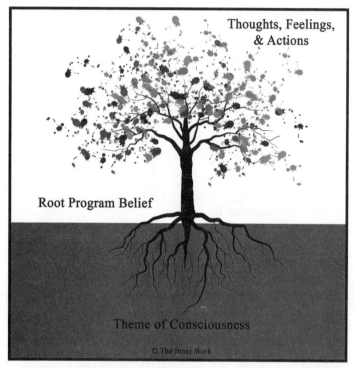

Examples:

Thought: "I am right about this. They are wrong."

Feeling: Prideful

Action: Argumentative

Root Program Belief: I believe I am superior and others are inferior.

Theme of consciousness: Insecurity

Thought: "I want him. I want to get his attention."

Feeling: Craving

Action: Seduction

Root Program Belief: I believe when I am wanted—I am loved.

Theme of consciousness: Inadequacy

Thought: "I look stupid, they are probably laughing at me."

Feeling: Humiliation

Action: Repress and hide

Root Program Belief: I'm unlovable.

Theme of consciousness: Rejection

Thought: "My life will never be as good again. Life is so tragic."

Feeling: Sadness

Action: Sulk

Root Program Belief: I lose everything I love.

Theme of consciousness: Loss

Thought: "I will get revenge. I'll show them."

Feeling: Aggression

Action: Attack or demean

Root Program Belief: I expect to get what I want.

Theme of Consciousness: Violation

Everything is Rooted in a Theme of Consciousness

These examples can help you begin to understand the depth and meaning behind your habitual thoughts and feelings. Nothing is mundane, and everything is always revealing an underlying theme of consciousness. One of the most direct ways to identify a theme is to question the motivation and intention behind your thoughts, words, and actions. Without conscious awareness of why we think what we think or do what we do, we can go our entire lives carrying around limiting programs of the past that are not serving us—unknowingly allowing them to influence who we are in the present. And these inherited themes will ripple into multiple aspects of our lives. For example, in the wound of insecurity, not only will we experience arrogant thoughts and have feelings of superiority and pridefulness, but we will most likely be attracted to art, movies, and music that promote egotism. Like goes with like, thus each theme will attract people, places, and circumstances that match its vibrational frequency.

Just as thoughts are not intrinsically who we are and are a byproduct of a theme of consciousness, so too are personality traits and preferences. For instance, preferring a loud bar over a quiet temple is correlated to the theme of consciousness our soul is occupying. So is choosing to smoke cigarettes or abstaining, eating healthy or not, enjoying our career or resenting it, being confrontational or easy-going, etc. And this can be said for just about everything we claim as "just who I am." Within our personality, what we might have once thought was rigid and fixed is actually all subject to change and can evolve. Anything is possible.

To transcend a theme that is no longer serving you and move into a theme that does, you must stop compartmentalizing your life. There is no situation, reaction, or scenario that is isolated from your anatomy of consciousness at that moment. Everything is connected. How you do anything is a reflection of how you do everything. By looking for recurring patterns, you can start to identify the frequencies you are living in. If you are living in love, faith and trust will come out of you even in times of struggle. If you are living in distrust, fear will come out of you no matter how ideal your conditions become. The circumstance is not responsible for your experience; your theme of consciousness is.

When looking at humanity with the knowledge of the themes of consciousness, it will become clear that the reason we see so much conflict and turmoil in the world, and throughout history, is due to these vastly varying themes of consciousness all interacting with each other while experiencing completely different paradigms of reality. Thus from one theme, what is seen as completely "right" is actually "wrong" from another. Just like a hologram from different perspectives reveals completely different images, so it is with this human experience of life. We all may be looking at the same world or be sharing the exact same situation, but how we each experience it is drastically different. We refer to this as **paradigm blindness**. As much as we like to think there is a fixed, objective world that is separate from us, in truth, objectivity is in the eye of the beholder. This has now been confirmed through discoveries in quantum physics, i.e., the collapse of the wave function.

Anything that is outside the boundaries of our familiar spectrum of consciousness will trigger the ego to respond with confusion or defensiveness. For example, to someone with wounds of violation or insecurity, a concept such as surrender will seem foolish and incomprehensible. Likewise, to those struggling with judgement, forgiveness of self and others is really hard to do and almost feels unacceptable, implausible, or even impossible. Therefore, our anatomy of consciousness sets up not only the possibilities for our life but also our limitations.

Behind every action is a motivation that is rooted in a theme of consciousness. True freedom and lasting happiness can never be realized in gratifying the ego-mind's demands to adhere to its limiting programs. Inner peace can only be experienced outside the confines of a programmed mind. While the themes of consciousness completely color our perception of reality, it is important to realize that all options are technically always available to us. We can view the hologram from whichever vantage point we wish; just know that each view, or theme, is very different in its degrees of freedom and happiness. So the question then becomes which ones are most enjoyable?

In order to move out of a deeply rooted theme of consciousness, you will need to live the practice of *Inner Work*. In every single moment, you have a choice to either stay obedient to an old program or to break free of it and choose anew.

"People try so hard to let go of their negative behaviors and
thoughts, and it doesn't work, or it works, but only for a short time.
I didn't let go of my negative thoughts,
I questioned them, and then they let go of me."
- Byron Katie

Overcoming Negativity

When we become self-aware, we can honestly examine and question our ego's patterns from a place of nonattachment. What we may discover is that it actually enjoys its negative beliefs. As strange as it may seem, our ego has convinced us there is a payoff from maintaining negativity and dissatisfaction with life. There is a false sense of power, security, and control in being able to resist life and be negative. It is also the easiest thing to do.

It is easy to complain; it is a worthy challenge to be consistently grateful. It is easy to be unhappy. It takes courage to see the perfection of everything *as it is*. It requires great discipline and faith to maintain a positive attitude in the face of hardship. It takes true power to overcome the negativity of our own ego and others', and awaken to being happy, fulfilled, and compassionate. You are capable of rising to this challenge—in fact, it is your destiny or else you wouldn't be *here now*.

Our misery has actually just been a reflection of the ego's narcissism and a demonstration that it would rather complain, throw tantrums, and kick and scream about our life instead of doing anything to change its perspective. In a delusional way, our ego convinces us that being miserable and depressed is secretly empowering. It subconsciously believes, "If I can't control my life, at least I can control my *resistance* to it." Thus the ego makes things even more difficult than they need to be. From a different theme of consciousness, under the exact same hardships, it is possible to maintain optimism and be loving despite the situation, thereby demonstrating true power. It is important to note that the themes below accountability rely on force, whereas the themes from accountability upward rely on the power of love. Force resists life; true power affirms it.

For example, in the wound of rejection, the ego will look for any situation to validate how worthless it is, "See, I told you this would happen, nothing ever works out for me. Pathetic. I am so unlucky and worthless." Judgement might complain, "God must be punishing me. I probably deserve this. This is what I get. Everything is against me. It's their fault." Or perhaps in the wound of inadequacy, it thinks, "No matter how hard I work, I never seem to get ahead. The more I want things, the more life shows me I can't have it."

The ego actually believes its suffering is proving a point. But the only point it is proving is how confused it is. If not careful, the ego can actually become enthusiastic about proving how awful our life is, which is a fascinating discovery. Notice that people often gather to complain and share their stories of hardship and loss, almost as if in a competition of, "Whose is worse?" The adage really is true that misery loves company, and if we want to find peace in life, we have to step back and start questioning our ego's perspectives and agendas.

"If you must doubt something, doubt your limits."
- Bob Proctor

The Possibility of Change

This flirtation with suffering and darkness is to be expected and does not make us sick or twisted—simply naive. We all inherited a limited human ego that is attached to familiarity—regardless of if it is beneficial for us or not. Because our mental stories have become so familiar to us, our brain actually becomes accustomed to the emotions and chemicals those particular types of thoughts produce. For example, fearful or aggressive thoughts release adrenaline. Worrisome and stressful thoughts produce cortisol—another very powerful hormone.

Over time, our bodies and brain start to crave and expect these chemicals on a regular basis. In some extreme cases we can become literally addicted to our stress, our suffering, or our victimization. Understand it will take time and consistent practice of *Inner Work* to rewire the brain's neurochemistry. Be patient, kind, and compassionate with yourself. Over time the old needs and negative energy cravings of the brain and body will subside. And eventually, instead of craving stress hormones from worry and doubt, your body and brain will want to enjoy the endorphins that come with gratitude. To trust in goodness and have faith and hope in a brighter future elicits its own spiritual, mental, and physical rewards simply by indulging in such energies of optimism.

"The more you engage in any type of emotion or behavior, the greater your desire for it will become."
- Chris Prentiss

If true happiness and inner peace are rare, it is not because it isn't available but rather because few have chosen it. Happiness and inner peace are hallmarks of your natural state; they are who you truly are. The ego is just blocking you from realizing it and has convinced you that you can't have them or that they are only found somewhere other than right now. The truth is always simple. The ultimate choice is always present in every moment.

All themes of consciousness can be transmuted and healed. No one is exempt. All of us are forgiven in the moment of sincere acknowledgment. All are loved no matter what. No one is forsaken. Nothing is off-limits. If you want to be truly happy, you *can* do this. Everyone can be happy and fulfilled. True freedom and lasting happiness are just a continuous lifestyle choice that transcends the wounded themes of consciousness. There's nothing more to it—we don't have to make it more complicated. It is not something that is earned from accomplishing rare, "challenging" things. Nothing needs to be earned or gained, only *remembered* through *surrendering* resistance to the truth. The truth is that you are loved beyond possible comprehension and have equal access to true freedom and lasting happiness. You have to let go of and stop listening to all the reasons your ego uses to convince you that you aren't worthy and can't have it.

Chapter 8

Practicing *The Inner Work*

*"Using awareness, personal responsibility, and inner work to
review our unskillful or frightened reactions, we become more
adept at turning habitual reactions to balanced responses.
These moments are very exciting and gratifying."*
- Bishop John Earle

The purpose of *The Inner Work* is to realign yourself with love and joy in every new moment and therefore live in an awakened state as your true Self. The first step to actualizing this is to become aware of any shift away from inner peace and gratitude first and foremost. Remember that your true Self is in silent bliss of existence so anything other than divine presence is the ego editing your reality. Whatever pulls you out of this divine contentment is what we refer to as a **trigger**. A trigger reveals a limitation in our unconscious programming and is our first clue on the path to freedom. **As a caveat, where this concept does not apply is in rare instances of abuse or any form of direct violation. In which case, the first priority is securing physical and emotional safety.** However, most triggers occur in our everyday mundane moments of life and reveal opportunities for self-examination and introspection.

Each time we are pulled out of peace, we must turn our gaze away from the scenario and instead look within ourselves with curious eyes. For some of us, dissatisfaction may arise first thing in the morning with the sounding of the alarm clock. As soon as we wake up, feelings of stress and frustration regarding our to-do lists may immediately come to our attention. For others, bitterness or anger may arise suddenly when our partner says or does something we deem inconsiderate or annoying. Or perhaps joy leaves us when an unexpected bill arrives, reminding us of a perceived burden. Whatever the initial fall from peace may have been triggered *by*, we must move our attention away from the circumstance and become more interested as to *why* we are even bothered to begin with. What belief is behind the trigger; what is the story? The purpose of identifying triggers is to connect them to a root program belief that is not serving our highest Self. In so doing, we reclaim our power and authority over our responses to life.

For example, let's say your partner or child does something in a public setting that draws unwanted attention and you become embarrassed or anxious, therefore falling away from a peaceful state. Without *The Inner Work,* you might feel tempted to reprimand them or shame them with guilt. This is a typical auto-response of an unconscious program of embarrassment and feeling unlovable. The program seeks to perpetuate itself by blaming other people or circumstances for its discomfort while avoiding taking ownership that the program itself is the issue. How we react to triggers is very telling as to what program we might be running on. If we reprimand and degrade another, we probably struggle with shame. If we judge another, we most likely tend to harshly judge ourselves and therefore struggle with guilt. Essentially every time we are triggered, we are being invited to break free of an old program that is limiting our joy.

Apply *The Inner Work*, and this exact same scenario can become a golden opportunity for healing and transformation. With practice, rather than blaming someone else for embarrassing you, you will instead inquire as to why you are so easily embarrassed. This inner analysis may reveal an unconscious part of yourself that still struggles with self-acceptance and self-love. Which then might spark curiosity as to where you inherited this self-rejection in the first place—consequently revealing a memory of a parent shaming you as a child for embarrassing them. And thus, the moment you first covered yourself with a blanket is discovered. The color of that blanket just happens to be rejection. With this kind of awareness, you can now decide for yourself to take the layers of shame off, knowing that this limitation was projected onto you and does not need to be endorsed any longer. Once separate from it, you can finally feel freedom in your own skin. With *The Inner Work* everyone becomes our teachers and all triggers become opportunities to heal.

> *"Everything that irritates us about others,*
> *can lead us to an understanding of ourselves."*
> *- Carl Jung*

With this type of awareness about yourself, there arises an actual choice to let the program continue or to choose something different. Without awareness of the themes of consciousness, programs, or triggers, there is limited freedom and lack of choice because we remain focused on the external scenario and never look inside ourselves for the solution. Without realizing there is a choice in how we experience reality, we remain obedient to the voice inside our heads, forever finding ways to validate the very programs which keep us trapped.

It is with this new, heightened awareness of ourselves that the gap emerges between each situation and our response to it, thus allowing for genuine free will and decision. By becoming aware of our ability to choose our inner perspectives and beliefs in every moment, we reclaim authority over our lives and exercise our spiritual will to go beyond the ego's patterns of behavior and rewrite the root program.

Using the same example as above, with *The Inner Work*, you would *feel* embarrassment *arising,* and rather than becoming it, you could *observe* it.

The inner narrative changes from, "This *is* so embarrassing, *I am* so embarrassing," to "*a* feeling of embarrassment is coming up, but I choose peace. I am loved as I am. I can never be embarrassed and am always doing the best I can. I am perfect, whole, and complete. I embrace myself and love myself. Anyone's opinion of me has nothing to actually do with me."

> *"When the mind is disturbed by negative thoughts,*
> *one should dwell on their opposites."*
> *- The Yoga Sutras of Patanjali 2:33*

After affirming this new narrative, breathe into this new outlook, notice how much better it feels, how empowering it is, and how much more loving and *true* it feels. Settle into this new person you are becoming. Your transformation in these everyday moments is *real* and not to be brushed off as insignificant. True change is in the simple, small moments of life. There is nothing grandiose needed. All genuine healing comes from consistent, small moments that accumulate to make a powerful, lasting shift in awareness. Every time you consciously choose your new narrative over your inherited programs, you are literally becoming a new person biologically, mentally, and spiritually.

By uprooting and replacing old programs, you institute a new pattern of approach to your life, thereby altering every aspect of your life, such as levels of success, happiness, love, and feelings of connection and purpose. Gradually the old programs will stop being triggered because your mind will know they are no longer a viable option—imagine a program being uninstalled or deleted from a computer. Thus, with the old program removed and the new narrative established and reinforced, the new program will take root, and consciousness can move on in its evolution. This is how all true evolution and lasting change takes place.

There are only three simple steps to *The Inner Work* process that can be practiced throughout everyday moments: become aware of the trigger, connect them to a root program belief and theme of consciousness, then uproot and replace it with a new narrative of a higher perspective.

Step 1: Awareness of Triggers

The first step of your healing process is to become aware of any time you fall from a state of peace and contentment and ask yourself what exactly *triggered* such a change. Clearly identify the thoughts, feelings, or actions associated with the situation making you uncomfortable. What is *arising*? Take the focus off the external circumstance and focus purely on what's going on *within you*. Give it a name—anxiety is arising. Craving is arising. Insecurity is arising.

Whatever trigger you identify while examining yourself, look at it objectively and take note without judgment. It is helpful to observe the body and mind's behaviors and patterns *impersonally*. Remembering the impersonal nature of your inherited ego removes unnecessary judgment about it. Have courage to look at your triggers with the eyes of the observer, just witnessing all that being human entails. Awareness is the first step in the healing process. Once you identify a trigger, you can identity the root program belief that generated the trigger.

Step 2: Identify the Root Program Belief & Theme of Consciousness

Now that there is awareness around the trigger, you can begin the uprooting and healing process. First, reflect on the trigger you have identified. Then, become curious as to what this trigger is *actually* revealing? What deeper belief is being ruffled and brought to the surface? Instead of following your mind down the rabbit hole of blame and rationalization, inquire as to what the trigger says about *yourself* instead.

Can you identify any patterns with this particular thought, feeling, or action? Have you experienced this trigger before? Is this connected to past traumas or memories? Does it get triggered often? Start to connect the dots. Remember, nothing is isolated.

Triggers will always reveal deeply rooted beliefs about your life and who you think you are. Avoid blaming your thoughts, feelings, or actions on the current situation, circumstances, or other people. Use "I" language instead to take the focus away from the external and into the internal, thus exposing the theme of consciousness you are occupying. The external trigger did not "make" you fall from peace; it may be an uncomfortable or even painful situation, but your response to the trigger is always your free choice. Now is your chance to implement honest self-inquiry of *your own* reactions to the trigger. Without self-reflection, you will continue to focus on the external event and never reveal the true source of your suffering, which is much deeper and entirely internal. You can't remove a tree by trimming its leaves; you have to dig out the root.

It's important to note that finding the root is not to perpetuate blame or victimhood further. It is simply to help you understand that all negative root program beliefs are inherited, limited perceptions from past wounds that are still influencing your present. Once the root is identified, it makes it easier to let the story go and replace it with something you'd like to experience *now*. Thus allowing the possibility to truly change your life and experience the present moment free from the influence of limiting root program beliefs.

Trigger: Anxiety is arising.

Root Program Belief: I believe the worst case scenario is going to happen to me. I've been hurt in the past and now I'm assuming I'll keep getting hurt.

Theme of Consciousness: This must be coming from distrust.

Trigger: Craving is arising.

Root Program Belief: I believe I will only be satisfied once I get what I want. In the past I coped with my vulnerabilities by indulging in food, materialism, drugs, alcohol, or sex and now am assuming they are the source of my confidence.

Theme of Consciousness: This must be coming from inadequacy.

Trigger: Competitiveness is arising.

Root Program Belief: I believe I am not liked or loved unless I prove my worth. I felt inferior when I lost, or was overlooked in the past, and now I am assuming that if I am not the best, or a "winner," I will not be loved.

Theme of Consciousness: This must be coming from insecurity.

Step 3: Release & Replace

Once the root program belief and theme of consciousness are exposed, the next question is, do you want to continue the narrative or rewrite it? Do you want to continue to live in the wounds of rejection, judgement, overwhelm, loss, distrust, inadequacy, violation, or insecurity? Whatever theme of consciousness is revealed, if it is bringing you suffering or limitation, it is time to let it go.

The third step is all about the pause between the situation and your response to it. Breathe into the gap. You *do* have a choice to *respond* differently than you have in the past. It is within this gap that you can actually make a conscious choice to "reprogram" and restore the mind back to the theme of true freedom and lasting happiness—its original, pure nature. If a belief does not feel like the most loving perspective you could take, then it is best not to indulge in it and choose differently. Leave your old programs in the past and refrain from bringing them into the present. Release the old root program belief with a new narrative that is in alignment with your true Self. Every passing experience of your life is another chance to turn it all around. You don't have to go another minute carrying the baggage and limitations of your past.

Trigger: Anxiety is arising.

Root Program Belief: I believe the worst case scenario is going to happen to me. I've been hurt in the past and now I'm assuming I'll keep getting hurt.

Theme of Consciousness: This must be coming from distrust.

New Narrative: It is also possible the best case scenario will happen. My past does not define me. I will always be okay and am being guided. All perceived setbacks are actually working out for my benefit in the long run. I trust and believe in the goodness of life. Anything is possible for me.

Trigger: Craving is arising.

Root Program Belief: I believe I will only be satisfied once I get what I want. In the past I coped with my vulnerabilities by indulging in food, materialism, drugs, alcohol, or sex and now am assuming they are the source of my confidence.

Theme of Consciousness: This must be coming from inadequacy.

New Narrative: **What I desire is actually within me. I am tired of my cravings controlling my mood. I am ready to make a change. I will break free of this. I am free, I am whole, I am complete. I am disciplined over my impulses.**

Trigger: Competitiveness is arising.

Root Program Belief: I believe I am not liked or loved unless I prove my worth. I felt inferior when I lost, or was overlooked in the past, and now I am assuming that if I am not the best, or a "winner," I will not be loved.

Theme of Consciousness: This must be coming from insecurity.

New Narrative: **I am always loved unconditionally. There is enough love and happiness for everyone. There is no actual competition to be me. I have nothing to prove. I do not need to earn love, for I am *innately* loved. Love is my natural, effortless state and is within me.**

Every time you follow through on this process, you are being reborn anew. As you consciously change your internal responses to life, your brain and body will follow the spiritual will's intentions. Trust the infinite power of your consciousness that aligns and molds your entire experience of your physical reality. With time, the brain's neurochemistry will begin reconstructing itself to match the new theme of consciousness you are endorsing. The stronger the attachment, the longer it may take to rewire—but it *can* be done through consistent effort.

The Inner Work is a contemplative lifestyle practice that brings powerful change through everyday, mundane moments that hold infinite potential. Nothing extravagant is necessary; your ability to change, evolve, and adapt is within your hands in every moment. Each time you embrace your new narratives with courage and trust, the entire universe shifts to reflect back your newly awakened Self. With every conscious redirection of your focus away from your past programs, you are re-sowing the fields of your consciousness and harvesting a new crop. Thus bringing forth new root program beliefs and therefore thoughts, feelings, and actions of your liberated Self. This process of awakening can be gradual or instantaneous; it's all a matter of your faith and ability to *let go* and *surrender* resistance to remembering *who you really are*.

Chapter 9

Healing the Wounded Themes of Consciousness

"Accept responsibility for your life.
Know that it is you
who will get you to where you want to go, no one else."
- Les Brown

The following chapters have been prepared for you to use as a practical *how-to* guide throughout your *Inner Work* journey. Each theme will be outlined to show common triggers, traumas, root programs, defense mechanisms, overall view of life, and how to heal them. Use these chapters to help you identify the themes of consciousness for yourself and build awareness of where you find yourself getting stuck. When exploring the wounded themes of consciousness, it is important to note that they represent layers of *resistance* to accepting our true nature of unconditional love. They represent who we are *not*. We are already, and always have been, loved and innocent; it is only the wounded themes of consciousness that blind us from this truth, like clouds blocking the sun.

Because the themes of consciousness are a spectrum, there will be certain ones that you find your ego is more attached to than others based on its conditioning. You'll also notice that there are certain themes you are at peace with already. It is possible for you to spend most of your time in a liberating theme, such as accountability or self-motivation, but periodically still struggle with an unhealed wound of insecurity or judgement. You may also find that you experience different themes in different areas of your life—for example, acceptance in your career but distrust when it comes to relationships and love.

It is important to clarify that experiencing the wounded themes of consciousness is a natural part of being human and none of them are better or worse than others. Allow yourself to be where you are with curiosity rather than judgement. Feeling your feelings fully *is* what brings about healing. Suffering comes from stuck emotions—either through attachment and identification with them as who we think we are or by bypassing and avoiding them. In fact, all defense mechanisms, or side effects of unreconciled wounds are created by either *overcompensating* to mask our pain or *avoiding* feeling our pain.

As a final caveat, be compassionate with yourself regarding anything you may discover and remember that the ego is not personal and has been attaching itself to limitations innocently without knowing any better. You are *not* your ego's attachments and resistances. We're all in this together. You can do this!

THEMES OF WOUNDING

3D Reality

Sᴇʟꜰ Aꜱ Bᴏᴅʏ

SUFFERING

Victim/Abuser Mentality

INSECURITY

VIOLATION

INADEQUACY

DISTRUST

LOSS

OVERWHELM

JUDGEMENT

REJECTION

As we progress through each theme of consciousness we encourage you to evaluate the degree of exposure you may or may not have with each theme. Assess the relevance, degree, and regularity you have with each theme's associated beliefs, traumas, triggers, or thoughts. Fill in your own spectrum of consciousness appropriately.

How to fill out your spectrum of consciousness:

Keep the theme blank if you feel you never spend time in its energy. Fill in the theme one node if you feel you rarely experience the accompanying beliefs, traumas, triggers, or thoughts. Fill in two nodes if you experience them sometimes. Fill in three nodes if you experience them often. And fill in the theme completely if you experience them consistently.

0 = never
1 = rarely
2 = sometimes
3 = often
4 = consistently

If you prefer a printable spectrum of consciousness, you can download a copy at theinnerwork.com/media

SPECTRUM OF WOUNDING

0 = NEVER | 1 = RARELY | 2 = SOMETIMES | 3 = OFTEN | 4 = CONSISTENTLY

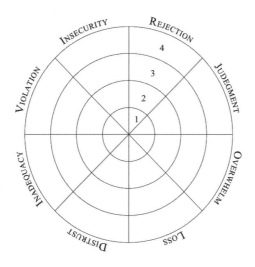

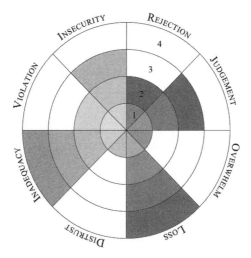

Wound of Rejection

TRIGGER:

  Rejection

ROOT PROGRAM:

  I am unlovable

TRAUMAS:

  Physical abuse

  Emotional/mental abuse

  Humiliation

  Racism/Prejudice

  Religious severity

  Harassment

  Divorce

  Abandonment

  Poverty

PRIMARY EMOTION:

  Shame

DEFENSE MECHANISM
OVERCOMPENSATING:

  Narcissism

  Pathological lying

  Recklessness

  Megalomania

  Criminal behavior

MEDIA CHOICES:

  Cancel culture

  Hate movements

  Crime/Abuse/Deviance

  Grotesque

  Dark

DEFENSE MECHANISM
AVOIDANT:

  Suicidal ideation

  Isolation

  Low self-esteem

  Psychosis

  Schizophrenia

  Drug/Alcohol abuse

INTERESTS/VALUES

  Nihilism/Atheism

  Superiority/Power

  Moral extremity

  Anarchy

  Self-harming

  Self-deprecating

PHYSICAL MANIFESTATION
EXAMPLES:

Acne: self-rejection

Anorexia: self-hatred

Thyroid: shame

Yeast Infection: self-denial

Seizures: rejecting reality

Upper-back pain: feeling rejected

THOUGHTS:

I am unworthy of love

I am not good enough

Everyone rejects me

I am ugly

I hate myself/my life

WHAT IT'S
TEACHING US:

Rejection of

abuse endured

Boundaries

APPROACH TO
CHALLENGES:

Seek to destroy

Seek to hurt

Self-harm

Lose control

Gaslight

Denial

HEALING:

I am innocent

I was projected

onto (abused)

AFFIRMATIONS:

It is healthy for me

to identify abuse

I give this shame

back to its sender

I am always worthy

of love

I matter

My life matters

Boundaries are

healthy

Overview

The most extreme of the mind's destructive beliefs is the delusion of shame. Shame stems from the lie that we are rejected, invalid, and beyond the graces of love and forgiveness. It believes itself to be unlovable, unwanted, a waste, and destined for an existence of suffering. Rejection represents the complete opposite of the Truth and is the ultimate forgetfulness of who we truly are. It can range from mild embarrassment, repression of our sexuality, racism, prejudice, all the way to feeling like the epitome of "evil" and cursed and rejected by Divinity/God.

The mind's story of shame is most likely stemming from a past experience of being rejected, abused, or neglected to some degree by a supposed loving figure, usually parents, society, or religion. Our innocent mind then believes itself to not be worthy of love and should be embarrassed and ashamed of itself or a particular aspect of the human condition that is being rejected, e.g., religion, race, ethnicity, gender, or sexual orientation.

In its mild form, rejection is taught to us by parents, friends, or society by telling us what we're allowed to be or not be. It is modeled through mocking our skin color, hairstyle, dress or appearance, unique gifts, personality traits, etc. To our impressionable mind, this teaches us that our innocent Self should be different from what it is, thus making us feel ashamed for being ourselves. Racism and all forms of discrimination are rooted in shame. Anyone who has suffered the trauma of direct or systemic racism will unfortunately, have wounds in this theme.

In religion, rejection may come from being taught to fear a God/Divinity that can reject, curse, and damn us to a fiery hell of torture. The misunderstanding that this causes is to believe that even an "All-Loving" God could reject us, thus creating an overwhelming feeling of worthlessness. However, nothing could be further from the Truth. Divinity's love is unconditional and always available, it is only the ego's rejection of this unconditional love that entraps and limits us and spreads the message of a rejecting Divinity. Through a trauma of rejection, the ego becomes attached to the belief of worthlessness and identifies with it. The mind then proceeds to push away anything that is loving and promoting innocence out of fear of being rejected by it again.

This wound, when taken to its extreme, drives all grotesque experiences of life; suicide, murder, genocide, rape, hate crimes, torture, etc. The ego in this wound believes itself to be above the law and rules don't apply to it because it is an exception. In a twisted form of narcissism, the ego of shame tests Divine Love by becoming completely vile in order to see if it will still be lovable. In this distortion rejection and trauma equal love. It therefore feels that it is loved through hurting others and deriving a sense of meaning, power, and worth because it can cause pain. Thus rejection represents the ego's desperation and cry for love by ironically trying to prove how *unloved* it is.

To overcompensate for the wound of rejection, it is possible to outwardly appear charismatic, charming, or "perfect" while secretly holding incredibly dark, selfish thoughts and hidden behavior, e.g., the charismatic psychopath or megalomaniac. The revealing feature of such presentations is that the ego cannot handle having its impulses blocked and will resort to extreme, self-deprecating behavior, such as hurting itself or others as an expression of thinking God, or life, is cursing it. It will reject all accountability and believes that any of its hurtful and unloving impulses should be loved and allowed without consequences.

However, because this is the theme of complete spiritual delusion, the most painful consequences stem from attachment to the wound of rejection. The ego tends to get itself rejected due to shameful choices. This creates a validation cycle of self-rejection and rejection from others. It is important to address any wounds of rejection we may be holding onto, no matter how insignificant we may feel they are, because the energy of shame is like a festering sore which slowly decays the soul if left unhealed.

Triggers

The wound of rejection will be triggered by anything traumatic, abusive, humiliating, or degrading. It is the theme of extreme trauma and the darkest of human experiences. While not all of us may struggle with its extreme expressions, we may experience rejection subtly in our subconscious, usually in the expression of embarrassment or any form of self-rejection, such as not liking our body.

Accompanying thoughts may sound like, "I am not good enough. God/Life cursed me. I'm so stupid. I'm incapable. I'm worthless. No one loves me. Everyone rejects me. I'm pathetic. I'm awful. I'm disgusting. I shouldn't have been born. I shouldn't be this way. God can't possibly love me. I will never be forgiven. I can't possibly still be lovable. I am evil. I am ugly. I am fat. I am vile. I am so sick. I am so demented. I am lost." If projected externally, the same thoughts will arise as, "*They* are so disgusting, ugly, worthless," and so on.

Healing

Due to the traumatic experiences the wound of rejection is usually spawned from, it can be extremely difficult to talk about or face. Thus out of defense, the mind denies, buries, and represses incidents of rejection—ultimately rejecting reality. This is due to internalizing trauma or shame rather than seeing it as a projection of the other person's theme of consciousness. The rejection we experienced from others is *not* personal *nor* true. The wound of rejection is only ignorance begetting ignorance—hurt people, hurting people. And because it is ignorance that creates rejection, everyone involved is actually innocent. This does not mean an abusers actions weren't a violation and don't need to be held accountable; it's a reminder that any trauma can only come from a traumatized source.

To let go of the wound of rejection and heal from its abuse, we have to replace it with compassionate understanding for ourselves and others. Those who rejected, traumatized, abused, or hurt us are only projecting their *own* rejections, traumas, abuse, or hurt. Our impressionable mind then made these painful projections *about us*, but it was never about us. We were, and always *are*, innocent. The wound of rejection subconsciously repeats cycles of abuse that were handed down to it. Thus abused people, tend to abuse others.

To heal, our traumas need to be put in our past as something that does not negatively define us. If we don't, similar scenarios as the original trauma will trigger the mind to think the trauma is still happening *now*, thus stealing our present as well. There needs to be a clear separation between what happened in the past and our new experiences, otherwise, we carry the trauma with us forever, i.e., PTSD.

Our innocence is still there and can never be taken—only temporarily hidden due to misidentification with the trauma of an experience. It is important to acknowledge this cycle so as not to go another day internalizing the rejection others projected onto us. We have to give it back in a sense, see the pain of the other person clearly—*they* have been rejected, abused, traumatized, or hurt and tried to pass it on to us. But we don't have to accept it. Therefore, we are their greatest teacher and mirror—only reflecting what is being rejected *within themselves*.

We *are* infinitely and unconditionally loved, even if those around us didn't know how to properly express it and ended up hurting us traumatically instead. To escape shame, the mind needs to cast blame onto its perpetrators in order to stop identifying with the energy of the experience. Setting healthy boundaries with our abusers is also necessary. And while this can temporarily move us out of self-sabotage and into the next theme of judgement, it is not the final solution. Whatever rejection we have felt due to others' projections, know that they were living with that same rejection themselves, probably even worse. They are not getting away with anything.

Our ultimate healing will eventually come through forgiving all those who wronged us in the past, therefore setting ourselves free. This will naturally arise later in our journey, for when we hold a grudge, we remain trapped in the cycles of rejection. In order to remember our own innocence, we have to also remember theirs. For as we do unto others, we do unto ourselves. While this may seem impossible at the moment, the freedom that comes through forgiving ourselves and others will naturally reveal itself as we transition through the themes of consciousness.

We can also heal the wound of rejection by helping and supporting others who have similar experiences. The greatest healers are ones who have endured suffering and turn their own traumatic experiences into wisdom for others' healing. Healed people, heal people.

New Narrative

I am innocent. I am always loved. I can never be beyond Divinity's love. I am pure. I am perfect as I am. I am always worthy of forgiveness and love. I am whole and complete, exactly as I am. I am loved even in my weakest moments. Others' opinions of me have nothing to do with me but are a reflection of themselves. Boundaries are healthy. Anyone projecting shame is living with their own shame. I give this shame back to its sender. It's healthy for me to identify my abusers. It is healthy for me to have boundaries with abusive people. I let go of the shame projected onto me. I love myself. I am divinely beautiful. I am loved as I am even with the traumatic experiences I have endured. My trauma does not negatively define me. I am accepted. Others want to love me. Others want to support me. Others want to see me happy. I matter to others. My existence matters. My life matters. My needs matter. My voice matters. I will not allow abuse any longer. I will speak my truth. I will accept my worth.

Wound of Judgement

TRIGGER:

Perceived mistakes

TRAUMAS:

Parental judgement

Religious punishment

Arbitrary punishments

Scolding/spanking

Public punishment

Choices as reflection of

worthiness of love

Sexual repression

MEDIA CHOICES:

Political

Religious

Polarizing

Guilty pleasures

INTERESTS/VALUES

Right and wrong

Good and bad

Politics and religion

Punishment, judgement

Righteousness

ROOT PROGRAM:

I am wrong

Others are wrong

PRIMARY EMOTION:

Guilt

DEFENSE MECHANISM

OVERCOMPENSATING:

Perfectionist

OCD

Black and white thinking

Harshly critical

Addictions

Bipolar

DEFENSE MECHANISM

AVOIDANT:

Blunted emotions

Repressed desires

Indecisive

Insecurity

People pleasing

Self-punishing

Prude

PHYSICAL MANIFESTATION
EXAMPLES:

    Canker sores: judging others

    STD's: sexual guilt

    Liver problems: harsh criticism

    Urinary Infection: casting blame

    Gall stones: guilting others

    Growths: holding grudges

THOUGHTS:

    I should have known better

    They should be punished

    I am wrong/they are wrong

    This is unforgivable

    I am being punished

WHAT IT'S
TEACHING US:

    Reflection on choices

    Genuine remorse/learning

APPROACH TO
CHALLENGES:

    Blame

    Project

    Harsh judgment

    Self-punishment

    Condemn

    Criticize

HEALING:

    Replace judgement
      with natural
      consequence

AFFIRMATIONS:

    It is okay to make
      mistakes

    I am doing my best

    I am always
      learning

    Natural
      consequences are
      not personal

Overview

In order to heal from the wound of rejection, we must see that its distortion was *projected* onto us. Thus the mind has to give the rejection back to its sender, which leads to judgment. The result of judgment, however, is guilt, which is why they go hand-in-hand.

The main difference between the wound of rejection and the wound of judgement is that rejection is about rejecting our fundamental sense of self as unlovable, while judgment is preoccupied with choices and punishment of "wrongness." While this theme of consciousness is still wounded, it is nevertheless a progression in empowerment out of self-rejection and victimization of shame that rejects accountability and consequences.

Healthy expressions of judgement cause us to learn from our mistakes so as not to repeat them. However, when it becomes an obsession of the mind, it is destructive, cruel, and harsh. The limiting beliefs of judgment do not allow joy into our lives because the standards for reaching or maintaining "perfection" are impossible and unrealistic.

Judgment is a self-imposed mental and spiritual torture in which we hold ourselves and others accountable to impossible standards. It pours salt in the wound and holds a crushing weight over us. Judgment doesn't let the past go, holds a grudge, and is unable to forgive itself or others. It clings to the flawed rationalization that we all should be "perfect" or "should know better." Any perception of a "mistake" is unacceptable. Judgment is obsessed with "should" and "should not," right and wrong, good and bad. All of these are defense mechanisms of the ego that it uses to protect itself from ever being hurt again—accidentally becoming the new source of its pain.

The root program belief behind all judgement stems from misunderstanding the difference between judgment and consequence. Judgment is partial, biased, and can only come from a limited, arbitrary perspective. Meanwhile, consequence is impartial, unconditional, and simply a natural, unbiased repercussion of making choices.

Judgment has been used as a force of manipulation for eons, through creating gods of judgment and wrath that we have to please, plead with, and seek forgiveness from, *or else*. All of it is a projection of our own ego-mind's fears and fantasies of self-rejection. None of it is actually happening—except in our own mind. The ego's guilt creates its own demons to fear judgment from and then projects them as coming from outside itself, especially in the form of religious misunderstandings of "God."

Somewhere in our lives, this belief of judgment, and therefore guilt, was inherited through the form of intimidation as a way of making us afraid of any sense of error. For example, being beaten, hurt, or threatened as punishment for doing something "wrong." Intellectually it manifests as fear of being seen as "stupid" or "less than" for making mistakes.

While the intentions of parents, teachers, or religions may have been "loving and innocent," unfortunately, the concept of judgment is flawed from the beginning and will only bring suffering. For judgment itself is another ego delusion, just like the shame and guilt it propagates.

Triggers

Due to the ego-mind's obsession with wrongness, all triggers associated with judgment will have to do with perceived mistakes. The ego may also overcompensate through obsession with being perfect in order to avoid or hide guilt. Its standards for everyday life will become impossible and unrealistic—no one will ever meet them. It will be staunch and brutal in its judgments of itself, others, and any perceived errors it projects onto—even judging the weather for what it should or shouldn't be.

Accompanying thoughts will be overly critical and unforgiving. Examples may sound like: "I should have known better. They should have known better. This is wrong. You are wrong. They are wrong. This is unacceptable. I deserve to be punished. I, they, or this is wrong for being this way. This is unforgivable. How could they? I hate sin. I hate evil. Sin/evil is wrong and shouldn't exist. They should be punished. I hate hypocrisy. There needs to be justice. This is so unjust. They broke the agreement. They disobeyed. This is immoral. I hate the unjust."

Healing

The only way to heal the wound of judgment is to surrender and admit that, as humans, we are not capable of making accurate judgments. The limited human mind has no idea why things are the way they are. It cannot grasp the infinite details of the universe and the eternal scale of existence and so must give up thinking it is capable of judging anything appropriately. Humility is the ultimate healer for this theme by surrendering the role of playing the judge.

Humility arises from accepting that we can't hold ourselves accountable for something we literally did not know at the time of our choice. Just because we understand the repercussions of our choices now does not mean we understood them accurately at the time of the choice. We are not capable of knowing the future and the infinite details of every choice we make. Lastly, even if we knew the wiser choice in the moment, we may have still lacked the strength and conviction to actually choose the higher choice. Thus we are always doing the best we can with what we are capable of doing at the time. Luckily, Divine Love's compassion is unconditional.

Because we are always innocent and unconditionally loved by Divinity, we are the only ones holding onto guilt; no one else is keeping tally. Everyone experiences the natural consequences of their own choices and determines their own eternal destiny through their spiritual, free will. From a higher perspective, there is nothing to actually forgive, and we are all innocent.

In a universe that is all connected and an extension of the same Source, we are all the same One. And therefore, to judge anything or anyone is to only judge ourselves. There is no judgment necessary in a universe that is innately perfect, balanced, and always harmonious. Consequence is eternally unfolding in every moment. It is only our limited point of view that creates judgments and perceives "wrongness" or "lack." Judgment is a perfect example of the mind creating enemies that don't actually exist.

The spiritual truth that judgment impersonates is actually consequence. Consequence just *is*. It is the natural repercussion of any choice or action. It doesn't require judgment; it is impartial and unbiased—like gravity. Therefore to make destructive choices is to attract to oneself destructive consequences. This is what all spiritual teachings are trying to convey: *all choices have consequences—not judgment.* Ironically, the consequence of judging another is to be subject to the torment of our own judgments. To project negativity onto others is to only attract the reciprocal negativity to ourselves. To believe in enemies is to *make* enemies. To condemn others is to condemn ourselves.

The most empowered choice then is to do our own *Inner Work* and take accountability for our *own* choices and stop worrying about others' actions. Let them work out their own destiny. All we have to do is focus on our own responses to life and the consequences they are creating for us. We are the only ones responsible for our spiritual destiny. Judgment, guilt, and blame bring only suffering. The unconditional, infinite love of Life responds equitably to our own choices, and we are all eternally free to choose for ourselves. Thus if we resist love, we suffer, if we accept love, we enjoy.

All guilt can be washed away in an instant if we could only accept our innocence and humility as humans. We are completely loved even as we make mistakes, which is so simple it is hard for the ego-mind to accept. Instead, the mind fantasizes that in order to heal our guilt, we must be punished or make some sort of sacrifice in order to be forgiven. This is not the absolute truth but is only a projection of how guilt views reality. From a more liberated, loving perspective, we do not need to earn forgiveness or love "back." We are *innately* loved and forgiven in every moment—we just need to stop resisting it.

All perceived mistakes, imperfection, or sin is only a reflection of innocent misunderstanding at the time, and natural consequence will follow every choice. There is perfect accountability and justice in the universe; there is no need for additional guilt that is self-destructive and causes even more suffering for self and others. Divine Love is ever-present and eternally flowing without condition or requirement. All we must do is *remember*, *allow,* and *accept* it.

We can let go of guilt by inviting a higher perspective of humility for our limitations. We are always doing the best we can with what we know and need not hold judgment over ourselves any longer. Focus solely on the present, what you can learn from your choices, and let the past go. Through consequence, we are deciding our new life trajectory in every new moment, and even as we make mistakes, we are always learning and recreating anew. *Now* is the only moment that actually exists. The past is not who we are anymore. We do not have to continue to drag it with us.

The way to transcend guilt and judgment is to let go of playing judge and allow natural consequences to unfold. Even if those consequences feel overwhelming to face. Find the lesson in the choices made and move forward implementing the newfound wisdom. Decide *right now* to become more loving, more forgiving, and more compassionate and it will be so. Invite and allow more love for yourself. Let the burden of guilt go.

New Narrative

I guess I just didn't know any better at the time. Seemed like a good idea at the time. I am always in the process of becoming. I'm doing the best I can right now. Others are always doing the best they can. I don't know someone else's story. I don't know the battles other people are facing. I don't know how deep this goes. I don't know the eternal scale of this situation. Everyone is doing the best they can with what they know. I grow through my mistakes. I am loved even as I make mistakes. God loves me. I am not wrong, only learning. I forgive myself and others. I am not my mistakes. I let go of grudges. I am perfect, whole, and complete even with my perceived mistakes. Mistakes are a part of the learning process. It's okay to make mistakes. It's okay for others to make mistakes. While my actions may have painful consequences, my soul is always innocent while learning.

Wound of Overwhelm

TRIGGER:

Inability to cope
and overwhelm

ROOT PROGRAM:

What's the point?

TRAUMAS:

Age inappropriate
responsibilities

Abuse

Life altering loss/change

Overwhelming
circumstances

Compounded negative
consequences

Poverty

PRIMARY EMOTION:

Hopelessness

DEFENSE MECHANISM
OVERCOMPENSATING:

Refuse to ask for help

Say "yes" even if they don't
have the capacity

Denial of limits

Self-sacrificing

MEDIA CHOICES:

Apathetic

Nihilistic

Sad stories

Melodramas

Depressive

DEFENSE MECHANISM
AVOIDANT:

Depression

Dissociation disorders

Detachment

Isolation

Anxiety

PTSD

INTERESTS/VALUES

The struggle of life

Burden of obligations

Disempowerment

Catatonia

Numbness

PHYSICAL MANIFESTATION
EXAMPLES:

Adrenal problems: hopelessness

Colds: overstimulated/over stressed

Gastritis: overwhelmed about future

Rounded shoulders: carrying too
much

Pneumonia: exhausted by life

APPROACH TO
CHALLENGES:

Shut down

Detach

Abandon hope

Take on more than
they can handle

Mental/physical
breakdown

THOUGHTS:

Why bother?

It's too much

I am incapable

I am a burden

Nothing will work

HEALING:

Allow feelings and
ask for help

AFFIRMATIONS:

I accept help

To feel is to heal

There *is* a way out

God/Divinity help
me

This will pass

WHAT IT'S
TEACHING US:

Realize limits, humility
to ask for help from others
or Higher Power

Overview

As consciousness heals from rejection and judgment, we may become apathetic and numb towards our situation because it seems too overwhelming to *feel* the weight of our choices or someone else's. While this is still obviously a limiting energy state, it is at least not preoccupied with hating and tearing itself and others down through judgment and rejection. Thus overwhelm blocks the unpleasant emotions of sadness or pain but also doesn't let itself be hopeful or optimistic about life either. Instead, overwhelm has now just given up altogether and doesn't know how to help itself. It has all become too much.

As a defense mechanism to cope with the overwhelm of life's tasks, facing consequences, past traumas, shame, or guilt, we may resort to a flat affect, a detachment to life, a lack of care or interest, boredom, and rejection of participation. In this state, we are not necessarily able to make a change, but we also don't have the energy to keep destroying our life. We just don't care at all. To the ego-mind trapped in overwhelm, everything is pointless, and nothing matters anymore. All common root beliefs that reinforce overwhelm will be regarding an inability to face reality, to take action and experience the consequences, or to feel our true emotions.

Triggers

Overwhelm may be triggered by any trauma, such as the loss of our sexual innocence, a spouse, a job, money, parents getting a divorce, parents dying, or getting in an accident and losing physical abilities. It can even be triggered by dwelling on the loss of time in our lives that we spent trapped in the wounds of rejection or judgement—thus it now seems pointless and "too late" to change now. Any loss that we are unable to cope with might trigger the mind to formulate an attachment to how hopeless life is.

The ego-mind won't want to do anything to seek change and instead only complain and wallow. It is the epitome of a "stick in the mud." In response to any solution, it will revert to thinking, "Why bother?" Everything feels too overwhelming. In extreme cases, the ego stuck in overwhelm will refuse to eat or take care of itself and may even become catatonic. The wound of overwhelm is apathetic and feels nothing as a way of coping.

Accompanying thoughts of overwhelm are things like, "Oh, it's *too* much! I just *can't* do it. I will probably just fail. It will probably all fall apart eventually. I'm incapable. I'm a burden. No one wants to help me. I'm an inconvenience. God doesn't care about me. Just leave me. Abandon hope. God won't help me. I'm dead weight. It's impossible. The odds are *too* against me. I shouldn't even try, there's no point. Nothing will work. It's hopeless. What's the point? I can't possibly face this. I feel nothing. I don't care."

Healing

The avoidance of sadness and the inability to ask for help is what perpetuates overwhelm. To heal the wound of overwhelm, we need to allow ourselves to feel and face the heavy emotions of grief and loss, which are natural to life. Accepting the weight of life's losses, or the consequences of our self-destructive habits, can be overwhelming yet is necessary in order to move forward in our healing and awaken our true power of a spiritual will. While the themes of judgement and rejection project blame for their situation, overwhelm is paralyzed at the thought of having to take accountability and own its responses to life's circumstances. Thus transition may require assistance from a higher energy field to help the mind shift into the beginning of building, or rebuilding its self-esteem.

We may need to call upon others for support, such as counseling, religious guidance, or the camaraderie of friendship or an anonymous group. Spiritually, we must invite and ask a Higher Power to give us strength and courage in order to face our situation. This invitation is essential because hopelessness, in and of itself, cannot possibly move forward on its own. To heal the wound of overwhelm, we have to reframe our perception of "loss" in the form of facing it through allowing grief and asking for help, even if it's just to ask for encouragement and to be reminded that we *can* do this.

Through our mere invitation and curiosity, we will find guidance out. All we must do is *allow.* There is nothing that needs to be "done"—thinking that moving on is something arduous will only reinforce overwhelm. All we have to do is ask, that's it. It is the humble prayer of the contrite soul, "God, if you exist, please help me through this." The "how" is not up to us. There *is* hope if we invite ourselves to see it. There *is* a light at the end of the tunnel. There *is* a way out. Anything could happen. We are never trapped and can always choose anew at any moment.

New Narrative

I can ask for help. There *is* a way out. God/Divinity give me strength. God/Divinity help me. I accept help. I accept guidance. It's okay to not know what to do. Anything could happen. I accept miracles could happen. I am open. I allow myself to be sad. I allow myself to cry and grieve. To feel is to heal. I'm going to be okay. I'm going to get through this. I can face this. This too shall pass. Others want to support me. I am not a burden. It's okay to be not okay. All will be revealed in due time. When I don't know what to do I can ask for help.

Wound of Loss

TRIGGER:

Perceived loss

ROOT PROGRAM:

Resist change

TRAUMAS:

Death

Loss of money

Unreconciled past regret

Painful unexpected change

Any and all extreme losses

Painful consequences from

 past choices

Aging

PRIMARY EMOTION:

Grief/Regret

DEFENSE MECHANISM
OVERCOMPENSATING:

Attachment disorders

Hoarding/clinging

Stuck in the past

Hysterical

Overly sentimental/dramatic

MEDIA CHOICES:

Tragic

Melodramatic

Romance

Underdog story

Loss of love

DEFENSE MECHANISM
AVOIDANT:

Emotionally cold

Calculated

Lack of empathy

Drug/Alcohol abuse

Denial of feelings

Inability to cry

INTERESTS/VALUES

Memories/past relationships

"The good old days"

What could have been

Missed opportunities

World tragedies

PHYSICAL MANIFESTATION
EXAMPLES:
  Colon: fear of loss
  Cramps: attachment
  Hands: clinging
  Lungs: sadness, unable to cope
  Heart issues: loss of love

THOUGHTS:
  I always lose
  It will never be the same
  I can't believe I did that
  I've lost so much
  What a tragedy

WHAT IT'S
TEACHING US:
  Natural grieving process
  Mourning with gratitude for time
    we did get (life is a gift)
  Impermanence adds to the
    the depth of love

APPROACH TO
CHALLENGES:
  Dramatic or
    detached
  Focus on regrets
    rather than
    solutions

HEALING:
  Face fear of
    impermanence
    and change

AFFIRMATIONS:
  I take nothing for
    granted
  Impermanence
    adds richness
    to life
  Change could be
    good
  I face the fear of
    the unknown

Overview

Once the stagnation of overwhelm is surrendered through the allowance of feelings and admittance of the need for help, the door will open to a higher theme of consciousness. Whereas in the wound of overwhelm there is detachment to life, grief allows itself to feel the sadness that accompanies trauma, loss, painful consequences, or change. The wound of loss is natural to experience as we traverse through the transitions of life, but when grief becomes habitual, it is crippling. It can make us feel regretful, depressed, and melancholic.

When we live in the wound of loss we become so tightly attached to the external world as a sense of identity that if anything changes, it triggers a deep sense of loss of self. Grief is a downside of the ego's *mineness* mentality because it attaches to that which is temporary. Thus the ego in the wound of loss views *all* change as a perpetual state of loss and lack. It only sees what it "loses" in each moment over what it is gaining. Therefore, we feel like we're always missing out and become regretful of our choices. Because of this, a common expression of grief is having a terrible time dealing with transitions.

The ego-mind when stuck in the wound of loss, projects that any change, death, or loss "should not" have happened and therefore resists the flow of life, sulking or regretting. Grief may express itself as feeling abandoned by others, Divinity, and life itself. This wound influences us to be attached, needy, and incapable of accepting that we will be okay despite circumstances constantly changing. So while we at least care about our life, which is a major step up from the numbness of overwhelm, we still tend to only focus on the tragic losses of life.

The beliefs that reinforce the wound of loss will all have to do with attachment of our sense of identity to something outside of ourselves. Thus the perceived loss is not about the actual thing itself but rather is threatening to the ego's livelihood, i.e., life without the object of attachment. The common thread, therefore, will be belief in our happiness, love, and sense of self as coming from "out there." This projection of value sets the ego up for inevitable loss and failure because life will *always* change, and nothing is permanent. By attaching our sense of identity to something temporal and fleeting, we become regretful and experience the pain and remorse of life.

Triggers

Because of its overemphasis on loss, triggers for grief will arise from anything where loss is perceived, whether it be losing an inanimate object, such as a piece of favored jewelry, loss of time, loss of money or status, or a loved one dying. All things having to do with attachment, abandonment, and codependency in relationships are signs of unhealed wounds with loss. All perceptions of loss and change will bring to the surface any attachments we have to the energy field of grief and regret. Ultimately grief will be attached to whatever it is we value the most: our time, people we love, money, possessions, ideal circumstances, pleasures, etc.

The ego habitually living in the wound of loss thinks and feels, "Oh, the pain of life. How tragic. I always lose. There is so much loss in the world. Who would I be without this? Why did they abandon me? Why did they leave me? Why did it have to end? Others only want me when it's convenient for them and then they move on. I'll never be the same. I can't possibly move on. I can't believe I did that. That was a waste of money. I can't believe I broke that. I can't believe I lost that. It could have been different if _____. I probably made the wrong choice. This always happens to me. I shouldn't have listened to them. I missed out. Life is so sad and depressing without _____. People always abandon me. Those poor people. What a sad situation. They lost so much."

Healing

To heal the wound of loss, we must face our fear of loss through accepting the inevitability of change and stepping into the fear of the unknown. All humanity experiences loss eventually; nothing is permanent. All things shall pass; no one is immune. Instead of getting stuck in grief, invite yourself to see the constant change of life actually adds richness, gratitude, and profound awe for all that is temporal. The depth of significance, meaning, and preciousness of life is elevated through honoring the fleeting nature of all things, *not* diminished.

When we *expect* change, we don't take life for granted and cherish it instead. Every moment is a sacred gift that we are not entitled to and is filled with far more passion and presence. Instead of seeing all that we "lose" in each moment, we instead affirm all that we are *also* "gaining" in each new moment. For if things never cease to leave, it also means life never ceases to *give*. Thus, we can let go knowing it all comes back around, life keeps flowing. Nothing is permanent, *including* grief. All things have a season. Death and change are a natural part of the cycle of life. When we allow grief to flow through us without attachment, we fully experience what it means to be human, care for others, and appreciate the preciousness of life.

The next level of transcendence is to release attachment to the external world as the source of our happiness and love. The love and joy we experience through people, places, and situations are actually coming from *within* us. The external world is just providing us an opportunity to *express* it. The perception of the loss itself is the actual limitation and source of suffering. In truth, no loss is possible. Ultimately the fear we must face is the unknown of what life would be like without our grief and regret.

New Narrative

This too shall pass—the good and the bad. I am grateful for every moment I get to enjoy. I take nothing for granted. Life is a gift. I am entitled to nothing. People, places, and experiences will come and go. I allow people the freedom to come in and out of my life and honor the precious time we have together. People are allowed to change their mind. I allow life to flow through me. I am present with this moment. Everything changes. I let go of my attachments. Things change for reasons I may never understand, but I trust in the goodness of life. I am excited for the transitions that come into my life. I look forward to change with optimism. I am grateful. No one can give me love, love is within me. I am not afraid to be alone.

Wound of Distrust

TRIGGER:

    The unknown

TRAUMAS:

    Physical violence

    Religious trauma

    Manipulation/Deceit

    Exposure to horror

    Doomsday culture

    Horrific accident

    Paranoid parenting

MEDIA CHOICES:

    Horror/Thrillers

    Crime

    Survival/death scenarios

    World news

    Catastrophes

    End of world

INTERESTS/VALUES

    Survival/safety

    Risk

    Future to fear and prepare for

    Worst case scenarios

ROOT PROGRAM:

    What if it goes wrong?

PRIMARY EMOTION:

    Fear

DEFENSE MECHANISM
OVERCOMPENSATING:

    Daredevil

    Survivalist

    Adrenaline junkie

    Doomsday prepper

    Risk taker

DEFENSE MECHANISM
AVOIDANT:

    OCD

    Superstitious

    Phobias

    Anxiety/paranoia

    Insomnia

    Risk averse

    Stress related disorders

PHYSICAL MANIFESTATION
EXAMPLES:

Breathing problems: paranoia

Diarrhea: worry

Foot problems: fear of moving
forward in life

Motion sickness: fear of not having
control

Lower back pain: fear of not having
enough financially

THOUGHTS:

What if it doesn't work out?

What if I get hurt?

People are out to get me

They have an ulterior motive

This is dangerous

WHAT IT'S
TEACHING US:

Healthy respect for caution

APPROACH TO
CHALLENGES:

Fight

Flight

Freeze

Fawn

HEALING:

What if the
unknown future
is desirable?

AFFIRMATIONS:

What if everything
works out?

I will always know
what to do in the
moment

What if I can trust
them?

Anything is
possible

Overview

To heal the wound of loss, we make peace with pain and grief and accept that life is always going to change. However, this then brings up fear of the unknown. Thus fear of an imaginary, negative future becomes the new obsession of the mind. Anything can happen suddenly that is out of our control, people can let us down or hurt us, and life could drastically change at any moment. Accepting this drives the ego-mind to become paralyzed with fear, fixate on avoiding fear, or become overly interested in testing the limits of fear.

Thus the wound of distrust pushes the ego to be overly concerned with trust, survival, competition, enemies, and security. It is worth noting that fear will actually feel like a source of energy and motivation in comparison to the previous themes such as rejection or overwhelm. Because the wound of distrust triggers the fight or flight response to survive, we experience a rush of adrenaline which is incredibly stimulating in comparison to the depressions of grief or hopelessness. Fear is motivated to escape or contend with its perceived threat in order to avoid pain or loss. Thus, this theme of consciousness feels more invested in life than the previous themes. For example, you have to be invested in life to be afraid of losing it. Therefore, while the wound of distrust is still a negative theme overall, in relation to the previous themes this will feel empowering and invigorating to "survive", worry, or test the limits.

The beliefs of distrust come from perceiving endless external enemies in the form of something or someone trying to take from it or hurt it. Yet, all enemies are projections of the mind's fear *as* the enemy. The ego-mind of fear is extremely suspicious, protective, defensive, and insecure. Its core beliefs are rooted in seeking security and the illusory promise of "safety" from loss. In order to attain that safety, it believes being anxious, paranoid, and doubtful will help. In its mild expression, it comes out in the form of social anxiety, fear of being lied to, fear of being abandoned, fear of being rejected, fear of failure, fear of loss, fear of getting sick, fear of injury, or fear of death.

As an overcompensation to the fear of survival, we may overly expose ourselves to things that evoke fear, such as constantly watching frightening movies, being a daredevil, a survivalist, or a thrill-seeker always tempting death—the ultimate fear. The adrenaline of fear can become highly addictive, and as it is continuously experienced the brain becomes desensitized, thus pushing us to seek more dangerous and scary experiences to get the same rush. Inadvertently, we become addicted to stress.

Triggers

The wound of distrust is triggered by fantasies of a dreadful future that may never occur. While the wound of loss is obsessed with regret, the past, and what it already lost, fear is now obsessed with what it *could* lose. Therefore fear swings to the other side of the spectrum living in hypothetical fantasies of a fearful future. The wound of distrust is also triggered by anything that sparks paranoia such as any perceived shady behavior in relationships, stories of scandals and deceit, the latest disease scare on the news or stories of murder—all promoting mistrust of other people and the world.

Accompanying thoughts of fear are things like, "What if _____ happens? What if it goes horribly wrong? What if I get hurt or die?

What if it doesn't work? What if they don't like me? What if I fail? What if I can't do it? What if they screw me over? What if I can't trust myself? This is dangerous. I'm probably going to get hurt. They are going to hurt me. He's lying. I can't trust her. People are out to get me. They want me to fail. What if I can't make it? They have ulterior motives. I might get sick. This is scary. I wonder if I can survive this? I'm so worried about _____."

Healing

While fear expressed as caution, rational planning for the future, and respect for danger is healthy and keeps us alive, fear as a habitual life-view will leave us constantly anxious about a negative future that may not ever exist. Thus to heal the wound of distrust, we must focus on motivating our actions through a *desire* for a brighter future, rather than out of *fear* of a negative one. This transition is made possible by accepting humbly that the mind does not, and can never, know what the actual future holds. Therefore all projections of a fearful fate are always only a fabrication within the mind. The present moment is all that actually exists and fear can only exist in the mind projecting to an imaginary future. Thus, both the grief over the past and fear of the future are illusions of the mind projecting outside of the *now* moment—the only moment there ever is.

The wound of distrust is healed by exploring the possibility that the future could, in fact, *also* bring desirable experiences *too*. This realization can only dawn on us by healing our wounds of distrust with ourselves. Ultimately, our greatest fear to face is our own fear of inadequacy. The mind of fear is so stuck on only thinking about what could go wrong that it forgets to also ask, "What if it goes right?" Therefore, we move past fear admitting humbly that we don't know what the future will hold, but we're open to exploring our desire for something better. We are open to finally learning to trust ourselves in our capabilities and our discernment. What if we are adequate and capable? What if we can handle life with all its uncertainties? What if we can trust ourselves?

New Narrative

Anything is possible. The mind cannot know the future. What if it goes right? What if it all works out? What if they love me? What if I *can* do it? What if it's even better than I imagined? What if I can trust them? What if I can trust my discernment? What if I can trust myself? What if people do support me? I am open to goodness coming to me. It could work out. I face my fears with courage. My skills and resourcefulness are adequate. I am capable. I am optimistic. I could get what I want. The future does not exist except for in my mind. I set myself free from the fearful stories in my mind. Fear is an illusion of the mind. I have access to all solutions and answers. I will know what to do in every moment. I will be guided. I will always be safe. I will always be protected. There is nothing to fear except fear itself. I trust myself.

Wound of Inadequacy

TRIGGER:

Perceived gain

ROOT PROGRAM:

I want, I need

TRAUMAS:

Being withheld from

Being teased/mocked

Not feeling desirable

Sexual trauma

Societal conditioning

Being objectified

Poverty

Comparison

PRIMARY EMOTION:

Desire

DEFENSE MECHANISM
OVERCOMPENSATING:

Addictions

Greed

Vanity

Histrionic personality
disorder

Attention seeking

Preoccupation with sex

Munchausen syndrome

MEDIA CHOICES:

Law of attraction

Wanderlust

Pornography

Status/celebrity

Social media envy

Clubbing/hook up culture

Pleasure seeking

DEFENSE MECHANISM
AVOIDANT:

Eating disorders

Repressed desires

Body dysmorphia

Secretive indulgences

Unsure of themselves

INTERESTS/VALUES

Sex/appearances/pleasure

Money/luxuries

Status

PHYSICAL MANIFESTATION
EXAMPLES:

Coughs: not feeling seen/heard

Aches: craving physical touch

Itching: wanting/craving

Reproductive organs: sexual issues

Tuberculosis: self-absorbed, envious

THOUGHTS:

I have to have it

I need more

___ then I'll be loved

I want to be desired

I want what they have

WHAT IT'S
TEACHING US:

Wanting more for our lives

Thriving, not just surviving

Moving beyond our fears

APPROACH TO
CHALLENGES:

Aversion to delayed
gratification

Spoiled tantrums

Turn to substances
to cope

HEALING:

Angry for change

Tired of wanting

Expectation for
things to improve

AFFIRMATIONS:

I am tired of
wanting

I will not accept
less

I am ready for
change

I'm tired of talking
about it, I'm ready
to take action

I will break free

Overview

As we open ourselves to the possibility that the future could also hold pleasurable experiences, and not *only* fearful ones, we become even more invested in life and start to *want*. Thus our energy, self-esteem, and engagement in life are drastically invigorated in this theme compared to those previous to it. Seeking pleasurable experiences in the form of desire can feel incredibly rewarding and satisfying to someone who started with wounds of rejection and once felt powerless. The energy of desire can be productive in the form of drive and motivation to create a better life for ourselves. As we shift our focus away from fear we begin to wonder what we are capable of. However, when our new found desire for goodness gets overemphasized it will become counterproductive in the form of greed, craving, and addiction because in the wound of inadequacy nothing is ever enough to fill the void we feel inside.

Similar to the wound of loss, the major blockages of the wound of inadequacy come from placing our happiness outside ourselves by projecting our self-esteem, love, and joy onto the objects we are desiring. In this wounding, we haven't yet realized a crucial truth: the satisfaction we seek doesn't solely come from acquiring the objects of our desires. Instead, it emanates from the self-esteem we cultivate in the process of achieving our desires. It's the sense of adequacy in our abilities to overcome challenges in order to achieve what we desire that is so rewarding.

While the previous themes were the preoccupation with *loss*, now the emphasis shifts to a focus on *gain*. Thus desire can become obsessive, lustful, and covetous. When the obsession with the desire leads to lack of control over ourselves, desire becomes enslaving. To know if our ego has become attached and addicted to a particular desire, take the object of desire away and see what comes up. If we are free, we will remain at peace; if not, we will either resort to a previous theme, such as grief and depression, or summon even more energy in the form of anger to force the object of desire back into our lives.

Another indicator is that when the object of desire is blocked or taken away, the addict will go about their entire day, week, or month not being present with what is happening *now*, but instead will be fantasizing about the next time they can get a *hit,* e.g. sex or pornography, drugs and alcohol, shopping, food, gambling, video games, etc.

When we allow excessive desire to make our decisions, such as greed and seeking gain at the expense of others, we inevitably bring only suffering for ourselves. The wound of inadequacy can even be a detriment to the community at large. Think of all the kings and wars throughout history—all fighting to please the desire for *more*. More power, more money, more territory, more status and fame, etc. It also demonstrates itself as the reckless, profiteering businesses that seek profit above all else, even at the expense of destroying the planet and hurting others. Unchecked desire is cancer—death by overconsumption, overpopulation, over pollution, extreme excess until the point of its own self-destruction.

The wound of inadequacy becomes enslaving by creating the belief that we are lacking *until* we fill the void of our desire. By projecting our security, love, and joy externally onto the object of our affection, we simultaneously give away our power and freedom, shackling ourselves to the object. The wound of inadequacy can never get enough or actually be satisfied and content. Therefore it cannot know true peace and security. Desire will always be chasing the horizon.

If we place our happiness in desire, our happiness will always be one more thing away: one more accomplishment, one more dollar, one more milestone, one more sexual conquest, one more *something*. Our security and sense of empowerment will forever elude us, always feeling like there is a hole and a lack. This is the source of all its suffering. The craving of addiction is coming from a deeper place of feeling incomplete, unloved, and inadequate. Thus the porn addict seeks to be desirable and wanted. The gambler seeks to be lucky and be favored. The alcoholic seeks to be carefree and beyond worries. All of these qualities are actually of the true Self, but the wound of inadequacy projects these qualities as coming from the external object, thus becoming indebted to it.

Through doing our *Inner Work* it is possible to enjoy feeling appreciated, complete, loved, favored, and carefree without needing the object of desire. Thus, in its healthy form, desire can be used to motivate the next stage in our evolution of consciousness, by wanting more for ourselves, for wanting true freedom and lasting happiness.

Triggers

Anything that causes us to seek self-worth and validation outside of ourselves will trigger the wound of inadequacy. This attachment can range from a mild expression of attention-seeking or wanting more money, all the way to extreme addictions to pleasure.

Common triggers will include things like status-seeking, lust, jealousy, pleasure of drugs and alcohol, gluttony, wanting to be rich, obsessing about being famous, obsession with success or materialism, or infatuation with being admired and acknowledged.

Accompanying thoughts of the wound of inadequacy may sound like, "I have to have it. I won't be satisfied until I get _____. I want it. I need it. I want more. I need more. I wish I had _____. I want what they have. I never have enough. How can I get more? Is he/she looking at me? Oh that's attractive, I want it. I want to be sexy. I want to be popular. I want better. I can't wait until _____. Give it to me now. How can I make this even more pleasurable?"

Healing

To heal the wound of inadequacy, we must recognize its never-content nature and its misunderstanding of how to access happiness. By placing our happiness onto the object of affection, desire infatuates us to completely overlook the fact that everything we are seeking is actually *internal*—to feel whole and complete.

Attachment to desire misses out on the *now* and is never grateful for what it already *does have* and how far it has already come. It only sees what is *next* and what is *more* desirable. Notice that soon after achieving a desire, it is quickly replaced with yet another one, and the chase begins all over again. In the moment of finally getting that high, that drink, that sex, that purchase, that fame, that job, that money, that _____, the elation eventually fades, and we are left unsatisfied—*again*. Thus no desire is found to ever actually bring lasting satisfaction or fill the void we feel inside. The mind will always convince us that maybe the next time will be different and crave more and better. Seeking happiness through objects of desire will inevitably leave us empty-handed because we ultimately misunderstand the fundamental, true nature of happiness.

In its constructive form, desire can be seen as a useful energy to motivate action, enjoy fun experiences, and set goals. Desire leads us to strive for more and seek the objects of our affection. However, it is not the object we are after but the unrealized aspects of ourselves that we *project onto the object*. For example, idolizing another for their beauty, wealth, or essence isn't a validation that they have what we lack and we need to *obtain it*. Quite the contrary, like a mirror, our object of affection is simply revealing what we wish to see or be *within ourselves*.

In its healthy expression, desire can point us in the direction of our true potential. If we can take the focus off obtaining the object of affection and use it instead as a clue that is pointing us in the direction of our own truth. When we see how this process works, we can break the cycle of yearning, longing, and craving and instead use our energy for actualizing and becoming the very thing we are grasping for.

Why is that we crave money, attraction, status, or power? Is it really to own and posses the material possessions? To be desired? Or is to feel a genuine sense of security and self-confidence? To live a life we feel we are deserving of? To reach our maximum potential and to be perceived the way we perceive ourselves?

Once we realize that what we are seeking in life is within us and therefore possible for us, we get frustrated that we aren't *being* it yet. We get tired and aggravated by the cycles of inadequacy and craving, thus we get angry for change and finally develop an expectation for a breakthrough.

New Narrative

I am adequate. I am already enough. I am ready for change. I am tired of accepting less. I am tired of wanting and craving. I will not accept less. I am frustrated for freedom from this cycle. I will break free. I am sick of talking about this, I am ready to do something about it. I am angry for a change. What am I projecting onto _____ that I'm not seeing in myself? I will actualize my potential. I expect to get what I want. I expect to be the person I really want to be. I am tired of being controlled by my circumstances. I am tired of not feeling good enough. I am tired of being controlled by my addictions. I will change this. I expect things to improve. I refuse anything less. My ability to learn, adapt, and evolve is the source of my adequacy. I can learn anything I need to in order to achieve what I want. I am perfectly capable already.

Wound of Violation

TRIGGER:

Unmet Expectations

ROOT PROGRAM:

I expect

TRAUMAS:

Restriction of freedom

Oppression

Violence

Disrespect

Autonomy violations

Physical violations

Boundaries being crossed

Expectations not met

PRIMARY EMOTION:

Anger

DEFENSE MECHANISM
OVERCOMPENSATING:

Aggressive

Violent

Defensive

Domineering

Power hungry

Argumentative/combative

MEDIA CHOICES:

Action

Violence/War

Power dynamics

Sarcasm

DEFENSE MECHANISM
AVOIDANT:

Passive aggressive

Bitter

Resentful

Spiteful

Complaining

Manipulative

INTERESTS/VALUES

Personal demands of life

Boundaries

Justice

Underdog prevailing

Freedom from oppression

Revenge

PHYSICAL MANIFESTATION
EXAMPLES:

Bad breath: gossip, revengeful

Bronchitis: verbal confrontation

Fever: burning anger

Infections: frustrations

Liver: consistent anger

THOUGHTS:

I will get what I want

Get out of my way

I'll do whatever I want

I didn't ask for your opinion

You can't control me

WHAT IT'S
TEACHING US:

Anger for positive change

Unwilling to accept limitations
within your control

APPROACH TO
CHALLENGES:

Violence

Aggressiveness

Yell

Grit teeth/resent

Put others in their
place

HEALING:

Surrender
expectations

Take pride in your
composure/actions

AFFIRMATIONS:

I respect myself
and others

True power handles
challenging
circumstances
with composure

I take pride in my
behavior

Overview

Whereas desire is consumed with desperation and *wanting*, anger, simply put, *expects*. Anger is no longer interested in yearning or craving; instead, it resorts to force in order to *ensure* its expectations are met. From the perspective of the wounded themes of consciousness, force is seen as "powerful" and impressive in comparison to the life-rejecting energies of guilt or shame. Thus to someone climbing out of the depths of hopelessness or fear, anger can feel intoxicating and even heroic.

Healthy expressions of anger can be used to motivate us to make changes and get unstuck, improve our situation, or work to improve the world at large. Anger becomes destructive, however, when it is sought as a sense of power. Anger uses *force*, which has to resist and fight with life—in order to feel in control. Meanwhile true *power* affirms life, is in harmony with the flow of life, and is supported through love and respect. Force is limited and needs external energy to keep it going, whereas true power is unlimited and has access to infinite energy.

The wound of violation is the theme of all impatience, aggression, violence, and rapacity. It is the infant throwing a tantrum and is actually unresolved sadness in an intimidating disguise. We perceive our unmet expectations as life not loving us and, therefore, anger over exaggerates situations and uses extreme language. Its entitlement turns into a delusion in which any obstacles or delays are viewed as violations and enemies *withholding* love. Likewise, we will perceive unexpected obligations as frustrating burdens that are trying to interfere with our goals. The wound of violation makes us stubborn, hard-headed, brutally unforgiving, and unable to let go of attachment to results. Thus the ego can become an extremist to the point of fighting and even killing for its goals and their illusory promise of gain and security. Ultimately the ego-mind stuck in the wound of violation is over-inflated in its god-complex, out of desperation, and subsequently feels *entitled* to its expectations.

Triggers

Anytime our expectations are not met or our boundaries are crossed, the wound of violation will be triggered. The mild expressions of the wound of violation are selfishness, entitlement, impatience, and frustration with our current situation or other people. When taken to its extreme, the wound of violation can cause us to be forceful and violent either physically or verbally. It will perceive enemies to contend with and destroy. It will be resistant, vengeful, explosive, and struggle with delayed gratification. It is impulsive and irrational. Examples of common triggers are things like becoming impatient with your boss or co-worker, being frustrated at your life and circumstances, arguing with your spouse, cut-throat behavior in business, seeking revenge for those who hurt you, passive-aggressive language, or road rage in traffic.

The wound of violation thinks, "I *will* get what I want. I will *take* what I want. Screw you. Get out of my way. I can do it faster. I will destroy you. You're expendable. You *never* help me. You *always* do this. You're taking *my* time. I don't care what you think. I'll do whatever *I* want. I didn't ask for your opinion. You're interrupting me. I'm about to explode. I'll get revenge. I'll teach you a lesson. Don't touch *my* things. Don't you dare get in my way. I will do whatever I need to get what I want. I'll make an example out of you. Nothing is going to stop me. I will end you. You can't control me."

Healing

To heal the wound of violation there must be a release of forcing control over others, circumstances, and outcomes. This is most successfully accomplished through building pride in ourselves and our ability to stay composed in the face of challenges and things we perceive as a violation. We have to loosen the choke hold on life, in a sense, and let go of the attachment to life *only* going *our way* and the delusional entitlement it propagates.

Instead, we must become curious about building true self-esteem that is able to maintain security even if our expectations aren't met. We must understand that anger uses force as a mask for hidden fear, whereas surrender of our expectations comes from the empowerment of self-confidence. We must develop healthy pride in our abilities to persevere, face, and overcome our trials.

Due to the paranoia caused by constantly having enemies to fight and burdens to overcome, the ego's self-esteem in the wound of violation is actually perpetually insecure and vulnerable. Thus, to heal this wound, we must realize that it is exhausting to constantly worry about our enemies, it is far more empowering to not create any in the first place. In order to achieve this we must learn to have healthy pride in our emotional composure and how we treat others, because it ultimately comes back around.

On the topic of power and respect, the wound of violation must learn that while it may have "won" and crushed all its perceived opponents, now it is alone and hated. No one respects or loves a tyrant. A person in the wound of violation, therefore, has to look for other ways to enjoy genuine self-esteem and learn to access true power through *lovingness* and *peace*. Thus, we continue onward in our evolution by focusing on our dignity, status, admiration, and healthy pride as a solution to gaining self-respect.

New Narrative

I let go of my expectations. I surrender and trust everything is working out for me—even this. I am loved even if things don't go according to how I expect. I go with the flow. Everything is exactly as it should be even if I can't see it yet. I respect others and their opinions. I can't control life, I can only control my response to it. I am patient. I am calm. I am at peace with or without my desired outcome. Being respectful is the most powerful approach. True power is secure and capable of handling things not going my way. True power is calm and composed. My peaceful nature is respected. I appreciate others. I can wait. There are no enemies. Nothing can take from me. I can handle whatever arises unexpectedly with composure. Nothing can withhold love from me. I am loved. I am secure. Security and worthiness of love are within me.

Wound of Insecurity

TRIGGER:

   Admiration and

   competition

ROOT PROGRAM:

   I am superior

TRAUMAS:

   Any previous traumas

   Delusional conditioning

    of entitlement

   Being told you are

    "chosen" above others

   Conditional love based

    on performance

   No consequences as child

PRIMARY EMOTION:

   Pride

DEFENSE MECHANISM
OVERCOMPENSATING:

   Denial of vulnerabilities

   Inflated ego

   Grandiosity

   Embellisher/exaggerative

   Superiority complex

   Arrogance

   Stubborn

MEDIA CHOICES:

   Rags to riches

   Power/money

   Status/celebrity

   Egotism

DEFENSE MECHANISM
AVOIDANT:

   Entitled

   Lazy

INTERESTS/VALUES

   Self-absorption

   Being better than others

   Competition

   Praise/admiration

   Status/accolades

   Delusional

   Spoiled

   All talk, no action

   Perpetual whining

PHYSICAL MANIFESTATION
EXAMPLES:

Stiff neck: stubbornness

Sciatica: hypocrisy

Muscle issues: resisting life

Broken bones: pride before the fall

Stuttering: insecurity

THOUGHTS:

I am the best

What's in it for me?

I deserve to get whatever I want

No one is as good as me

I am the smartest, other people
are dumb

WHAT IT'S
TEACHING US:

Healthy pride in ourselves for
overcoming the previous
wounded themes with honesty
and self-respect

APPROACH TO
CHALLENGES:

Denial

Competitiveness

Reverting to lower
themes when
triggered

Complain

HEALING:

Humility to face
vulnerabilities
with courage

AFFIRMATIONS:

There is no
competition to be
me

I face my
insecurities with
courage

Admitting my
weaknesses is my
greatest strength

We can all win

Overview

The wound of violation at its core, comes from sadness. It is ultimately begging for its expectations to be met in order to feel loved, heard, and secure. Thus pride emerges in an attempt to *prove* we are worthy of our expectations getting met. In its constructive form, pride comes forth as a genuine strengthening of the self-esteem and sense of capability in successfully facing the wounded themes of consciousness and the varying challenges of human life. It is able to face the darkness of shame and guilt, overcome the paralysis of overwhelm, accept the grief of loss, push through the fear of the unknown, and achieve desires. We become motivated and driven to be proud of ourselves and positively seek to feel admirable, respectable, and worthy. Thus the constructive energy of pride is absolutely uplifting and empowering in comparison to the initial energies of shame or guilt that seek to prove unworthiness.

On the other hand, the wound of insecurity can become overly emphasized and destructive due to its hidden vulnerabilities. In this wound we feel like we are not getting the respect and love we deserve or are entitled to. Thus as an overcompensation to *prove* and *guarantee* our worth, the ego-mind becomes inflated in its perception of itself and believes we are "superior" to others and more deserving. This superiority is used to validate why we *should* get our way, why our way is always right, best, and the most loved. People with the wound of insecurity, therefore, tend to become vain, self-serving, and appear egotistical. And while it is extremely motivated and driven, pride ultimately is only thinking of itself and is unable to celebrate others' victories or surrender in defeat.

The wound of insecurity comes from the other side of judgment. Whereas the previous themes focused on negative judgments of self and others, in the wound of insecurity, there is an over obsession with inflated, positive self-judgment and status. This is accomplished by denying any weaknesses, mistakes, or self-doubt we secretly have. Thus pride toots its own horn, boasts, gloats, and props itself up in order to feel good about itself. However, it is only the *presentation* of security and power, but in actuality, it is hiding unresolved vulnerabilities, which, if discovered, collapses the damaged ego back into shame and guilt.

The wound of insecurity is rooted in lack rather than the security of abundance which comes from accountability. As a result, the mind is ultimately trying to be better than others in order to make sure and get enough love. The root of the mind's story is that there is not enough love and respect to go around like a child fighting with siblings for mother's attention.

The wound of insecurity influences us to be in complete denial of our own weaknesses and human fallibility to the point of not seeing or accepting them even if clearly shown to us—our pride will *still* deny it! Because of this, pride is the epitome of ***paradigm blindness*** and, therefore, extremely dangerous because of its inability to face reality. Put simply, the wound of insecurity makes us believe if we don't acknowledge a problem, maybe it will go away on its own.

Pride goes before the fall because its own denial blocks it from seeing its weak spots and a healthy respect for boundaries. Thus people with the wound of insecurity can be reckless (due to denial) and over-committed (due to needing to "prove" their worthiness) eventually pushing to their own demise.

The wound of insecurity needs to feel the most *special and uniquely different* because it is actually still lacking true self-confidence. Therefore, when in the wound of insecurity, we become obsessed with credit-seeking and making sure everyone knows we are "right" and "best." Society has glamorized the vanities of pride throughout our history as epic, heroic, or impressive. Endless wars, competitions, and conquering of others, both on a large and small scale, are all examples of the arrogance of insecurity. From a higher awareness of love, there is no competition, which is a vanity of pride because there is nothing being withheld or in need of "proving." There is no lack and nothing to fight over. Everyone has equal access to divine self-worth, respect, happiness, love, and fulfillment *within* themselves —even with our weaknesses, mistakes, limitations, and humility.

Triggers

Due to pride's insecurity, its triggers will be anything related to earning respect and admiration. On the other side of the spectrum, the wound of insecurity can be triggered by humiliation and a perceived loss of respect. All we want is to be loved and seen, but instead of doing *Inner Work* with courage and looking at ourselves honestly, the wound of insecurity will try to manipulate respect from others through masking and lying. Thus, the wound of insecurity will come off as always in the know. It will try to be right, the smartest, the best, superior, the most loved, etc. It can range from expressing as the know-it-all or the entitled "spoiled brat" all the way to the grandiosity of believing itself to be a god that should be served and praised such the kings and pharaohs throughout history.

Accompanying thoughts for the wound of insecurity may include things like, "I am the best. What's in it for me? I deserve to get whatever I want. My opinion is always best. I know because... I am the most beautiful [or other valued quality]. I am right. My way is the best way. I am the most loved, they are not as loved. I am the smartest, they are dumb. People are stupid. I am right, they are wrong. I have the one and only way. I will go down in history. I'm perfect. I always win. I am superior, they are inferior. Reputation is everything. Everyone owes me. I don't owe anyone anything. I am the strongest, they are weak. I am the greatest ever. No one is as good as me."

It's denial will sound like, "I didn't do anything. I don't know what they are talking about—I'm fine. I didn't do that. That wasn't my intention. I don't believe what they are saying about me. I don't have to worry about that. They are wrong about my weaknesses. Nothing can stop me. I don't have to prepare for that. That isn't going to happen to me."

Healing

True security and unconditional love see that everyone can equally win, there is enough for everyone; there is no lack or shortage. There is no actual competition and therefore no need for delusional hierarchies of value, such as "superior" and "inferior" humans. All competition is a game of the mind in order to prove worthiness that isn't actually required. There is no competition to be *you*. You are the only one who can be you. No one can take true freedom and lasting happiness from you. No one can take your innate divine worth; it is yours and always will be—it cannot be altered or lost.

Real unconditional love and emotional security are powerful enough to "lose," surrender, and admit weaknesses, vulnerabilities, and limits without any loss of self-esteem. Likewise, when we are truly secure, we can also celebrate others' strengths and victories. Accepting the truth that we are *innately* unconditionally loved is not something to necessarily boast about either, because it is technically equally within everybody. It is not an accomplishment, only an *allowance and acceptance.*

We have to realize that ironically, when we have nothing to prove, we are usually in turn, respected. The most secure person has only everything to *give* and *share* and is a servant of love. When we remember we are always free and loved, we can't help but reflect that same love and openness to others and wish the same for them. We seek the betterment of our others because we know there is nothing lacking. Their benefit is our benefit. Our benefit is their benefit. A world of people genuinely happy and in love with life doesn't use up all the love so that there isn't any more left; on the contrary, it fills the world with even more joy and happiness without limit. Think of the last time you laughed with a friend or lover—*sharing joy, magnifies it.*

Thus the final step out of pride is made through accountability and humility. It takes courage and humility to admit our fears, insecurities, and mistakes, and through the revealing process of self-honesty, we develop true power and respect. As we summon the courage to face our vulnerabilities, we move into the positive, liberating themes of consciousness that bring empowerment, participation, purpose, meaning, love, and happiness to our lives.

Because insecurity is the fundamental core of the ego, it will be the greatest temptation to fall back into throughout all higher themes from here on. Thus as a caveat moving forward, we must be aware of pride coming back in disguised forms, such as credit-seeking, or forming an "intellectual or spiritual ego" and the pride of being "wiser," "more gifted," and "more spiritually mature" than others—which is a delusion. The ego will always try to identify with positive results as coming from *me*—*I* did this, *I* thought of that.

To avoid these pitfalls, we must realize that ***all progress is being given and not coming from the ego. We make progress despite the ego, not because of it.*** All egos will eventually be discovered to be an illusion. Underneath all egos, we are the same light of awareness that is the Divine Self; there is no actual better or worse, and therefore no separate ego to take credit for anything. It may be useful to recall that what we are really dealing with through our *Inner Work* is layers of *resistance* to the truth of who we really are rather than any sort of accomplishing or earning.

New Narrative

I take accountability for myself. Accountability is my greatest strength. There is no competition. I don't have to prove anything. I am humble. My life is a *gift*. All progress is a gift. I face my insecurities with courage. My vulnerability is powerful. There is enough for everyone. Others do not need to lose in order for me to win. We can all win. My way is just *one* way. I don't always need to be right. I am happy for others. I celebrate the success of others. I empower others. I enjoy others' victories. I use my abilities and talents to support and serve others. I do not need to *earn* love. I am *innately* loved. I give love to others. Love is my natural, effortless state. There is no shortage or lack of love. I build others up.

PART IV

A New Paradigm

Chapter 10

Accepting Our Destiny

*"The key to growth is the introduction
into higher dimensions of consciousness…"*
- Lao Tzu

If you have made it this far, may we be the first to say, "Congratulations!" and commend you on how incredible and glorious of a being you are! You have traversed through the most challenging of all human obstacles—we know it was not easy! No hero's journey through the darkness ever is. You have revealed the only "enemy" that ever existed and boldly faced your shadows squarely. You leaned into the discomfort of your ego's insecurities and courageously walked through them to the peace on the other side. We hope you are feeling more empowered and *present* in your life than ever before. We honor your bravery and the work you have done. You are truly marvelous!

As you navigate the themes of healing, it is important to note that while they are presented in a progression, they do not necessarily have to be experienced in a linear way. There is always the option to surrender directly back to love and faith, thus propelling yourself straight into a Spiritual Reality. It may be helpful, however, to see the gradual evolution of consciousness and the realizations which accompany each theme and help us transition into the next.

While the healing themes will feel positive and constructive in our lives, it is important to know that there is still so much more freedom and happiness to uncover if we remain curious to what else is possible. Thus we must accept our destiny of true freedom and lasting happiness and not get complacent and settle for any limitation to our freedom, joy, peace, love, and happiness. Always stay open to the possibility that it could keep getting *even better*!

As a caveat, as we master each theme of healing we take with us the benefits and gifts of each theme of consciousness while surrendering its limitations. The next step in healing and enlightenment is always relative to where we are. For example, there is a time and place for self-motivation in order to break free from attachment to complacency and ease, however, when attachment to results of our ambitions becomes a hinderance to self-acceptance we have to pivot our approach. What was once our medicine at one point in our journey can become a poison at another. This is why *The Inner Work* is a continuous contemplative lifestyle and not a destination because the journey is ever-evolving with us.

There's a reason we've been continuously reminding you to have courage throughout this journey. It takes incredible courage to do *Inner Work* and to put down our dissatisfaction with life and face the restrictions we have unknowingly accepted. As we emerge from the darkness of the wounded themes it is now time to cultivate true power and the energies of love and peace. It all starts with courage to be accountable.

"There are two sorts of courage. One is facing the cannon; the other is the courage of spiritual conviction."

- Vivekananda

THEMES OF HEALING

4D Reality

Self As Mind

RELIEF

Self-Empowered Mentality

UNDERSTANDING

ACCEPTANCE

SELF–MOTIVATION

EASE

ACCOUNTABILITY

SPECTRUM OF HEALING

0 = NEVER | 1= RARELY | 2 = SOMETIMES | 3= OFTEN | 4 = CONSISTENTLY

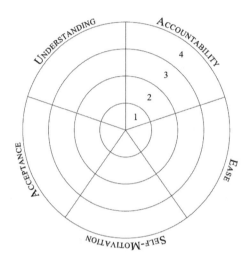

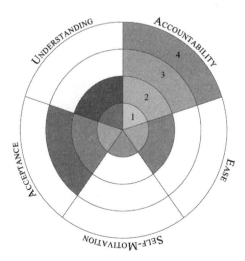

Accountability at a glance

ARCHETYPE:

The Honorable Warrior

ROOT PROGRAM:

Self-Honesty

TRIGGERS THAT KEEP US
STUCK HERE:

Duties to fulfill, wrongs
   to right, problems to solve

PRIMARY EMOTION:

Courage

WHAT IT'S WORKING ON:

Humility

HOW TO ACCESS
THIS THEME:

Ask if you're being
   accountable

Self-inventory, facing
   past defeats/shortfalls

Admitting past denials

Facing discomfort

Delayed gratification

MEDIA CHOICES:

Action Movies

Hero's Journey

Truth Telling

Healing

Freedom

Courage

PHYSICAL
MANIFESTATIONS:

Muscle development:
   inner strength/discipline

Improved health:
   accountability

Posture improvement:
   confidence

APPROACH TO
CHALLENGES:
  Do whatever it takes
    with honor and integrity

THOUGHTS/VALUES:
  My word is my bond
  I fulfill my duties
  Fight for what you believe
    is integrous/right
  Live with honor
  Protect innocence/freedom

TRANSCENDENCE:
  Stop finding things
    to contend with

AFFIRMATIONS TO
ASCEND:
  There is no one to contend
    with
  I have no enemies
  The world will handle itself
  Things will resolve
    themselves naturally
    overtime
  Everyone is on their
    own path
  I trust all is well

Overview

The wounded themes of consciousness all have to struggle to get what they want, whereas now, in accountability, there is access to love and true power. Wounded themes of consciousness resist life and reject love, whereas accountability courageously affirms life and accepts love, thus making it unlimited.

With the surrender of pride and the ability to admit ego insecurities comes one of the most monumental energy shifts into self-honesty and commitment to sincere improvement. Accountability is the theme that officially chooses good over evil, honesty over delusion, self-reflection over denial, affirmation over rejection, and Divinity over ego. In accountability, the human consciousness becomes truly empowered through integrity, courage, and dedication, as this is the theme of self-honesty. We accept, "I have to live with myself and face the consequences of the choices I make," and thus, it is the dawning of moral responsibility. What we do, and say, even when no one is looking, begins to matter to us. In accountability, there is bravery to unabashedly admit the ego's insecurities and fears while still moving forward.

While the wounds of inadequacy and insecurity fight for selfish intentions, the theme of accountability fights for others, to defend what it values, and upholds its responsibility to do what must be done. While pride and anger attack, courage defends. Courage honorably rises to the occasion to fulfill its duty with integrity, even if it means sacrificing itself for the cause. It is the energy of all commitment, determination, dedication, and productivity. Through accountability, we transcend the emotional insecurities of the human animal and tap into higher spiritual power of honesty and protection. Honor, respect, valor, and dedication to our responsibilities take precedence.

Accountability is motivated to action by something higher than itself, such as family, love of country, or God. It wants to fight for what it believes is right and good. It sees problems to solve and wrongs to right. It is obligated to act when it sees perceived injustice. Keeping its word and honoring its allegiances become guiding principles. Thus it lives for more than just itself and discovers the novel energy of love for the first time.

Accountability, therefore, is finally a constructive energy of life that affirms, gives back, and participates in society with dignity, honesty, and loyalty. Due to the belief that there's a battle to be fought in the first place, however, means there's still so much more peace and joy yet to be discovered.

Triggers That Keep Us Stuck Here

Ultimately accountability is still invested into the perceived battles of life, just with a better motive. Therefore it will be triggered by problems to solve, injustices to correct, wrongs to right, causes to stand up for, etc. It is driven by moral obligation and has to do what it feels is the good and right thing to do. Thus we contend within ourselves to be disciplined, as well as contend with others to protect our beliefs and values.

Accountability will think things like, "My word is my bond. Integrity is everything. I fulfill my duty. I face my fears. I live a life of honor. I can, I will, I must. Valor is respectable. Answer the call. Rise to the occasion. Discipline is key. Fight for what you believe in. Defend your family. Defend your values. Take accountability. People need to be protected. Do what's right. I am capable of handling my responsibilities. I slay my demons. I defend virtue. I stand up for goodness. I protect and serve. Evil needs to be stopped! Evil is the enemy! Everyone will be held accountable."

Transcendence

Because accountability lives in obligation, duty, and sees endless problems to solve, we ultimately miss out on the calm of ease that comes from a more balanced perspective. It is exhausting to constantly hold everyone and everything accountable, defend against perceived enemies, and try to fix everything. In order to release the limiting side effects of accountability, we must accept that life could be much more peaceful if we surrender the obligation to fight or right perceived wrongs. If we release attachment to the *need* to defend and hold accountable what the ego values, we can discover the ease of letting go. We can stop carrying the weight of the world and the need to change everything. However, this requires a greater level of trust and surrender because we must accept that the world will be okay without our input.

When it comes to our inner battle with our ego and the wounded themes of consciousness, transcendence of the limitations of accountability dawns as no longer needing to "defeat" the ego and face our insecurities but instead just watch it all as an impartial observer. The last step of our healing of the wounded themes of consciousness is to stop talking about them, stop focusing on them, or giving them attention. Accept that the battle is over and put down our weapons in a sense. In so doing, our shadows lose their power over us because we are no longer so reactive.

Courage must see that the more we participate and fight back, the more we polarize any issue—thus giving the opposition more strength with every push against it. From a higher perspective of love, an issue is not solved by destroying the problem, but by simply focusing only on the solution. If we don't create enemies in the first place, then there is nothing to contend with. As we stop being confrontational within ourselves and with others, we find a new level of equanimity that comes from no longer needing to "fix" or fight with anything.

New Narrative

There is no one to contend with. There is nothing to fix or change. Divinity's in control. I allow Divinity to handle the affairs of the world. Divinity will sort out all perceived injustices—that is not my responsibility. Nothing is going unnoticed. Goodness will prevail inevitably because it has no actual opposition. I have no enemies. I see only solutions. I am impartial. Everyone is doing their best with what they know. Everyone is innocent at their core. I don't need to argue. I can see everyone's point of view. I will stay out of it. I am neutral. I surrender. I put down my weapons. I do not need to be right. No one needs saving. Everyone is on their own path. I let go. All is well in the world. Everything is perfect as it is. I trust all is well.

Ease at a glance

ARCHETYPE:
   The Impartial

ROOT PROGRAM:
   Non-confrontational
   Maintain status-quo

TRIGGERS THAT KEEP US
STUCK HERE:
   Confrontation, more energy
      required, aspiration

PRIMARY EMOTION:
   Neutral

WHAT IT'S WORKING ON:
   Staying neutral
   Non-confrontational
   Simplicity
   Rest and relaxation
   Contentment
   Nothing to prove

HOW TO ACCESS
THIS THEME:
   Release the need to
      confront

MEDIA CHOICES:
   Simple Living
   Laid back
   Celebratory
   Back to nature

PHYSICAL
MANIFESTATIONS:
   Reduced blood pressure:
      reduced stress
   Improved digestion:
      reduced inflammation
   Dissolved muscle tension:
      reduced cortisol and
      adrenaline

APPROACH TO
CHALLENGES:
   Let life work itself out
   Relaxed confidence

THOUGHTS/VALUES:
   Live and let live
   It's none of my business
   I don't need to get involved
   I can handle changes

TRANSCENDENCE:
   Self-motivate to
     explore potential

AFFIRMATIONS TO
ASCEND:
   What else is possible?
   What am I capable of?
   How good can it get?
   I have unique talents and
     gifts to share with the
     world
   The more effort I put in
     the more reward I enjoy
   There is no limit to my love
     and happiness

Overview

Traversing through the wounded themes of consciousness can be an exhausting experience depending on our layers of trauma and how tight the ego clings. Due to this, there may emerge an attraction to the calm of not participating on either side anymore. The theme of ease knows the hardest and scariest part is over but we are not necessarily ready to keep exploring higher themes of consciousness either. Having the courage to look at ourselves honestly can be utterly terrifying and numbing to the ego. Thus to have made it this far is already absolutely remarkable and worthy of rest—especially if we had to begin our journey completely immersed in traumas of rejection. Ease is the feeling of, "The war is over—love prevailed. I don't want to fight ever again."

Thus after the courageous hero returns from the "inner battle" with the ego, we may want to find a neutral, passive resting state. The theme of ease is satisfied knowing there are no more enemies to fight and there is no need to be confrontational within ourselves or with others.

In the theme of ease, we reach a place where we don't need or have to change anything and can instead just remain uninvolved and trust innate consequence will take care of it. Accountability needs to solve problems, fix things, make changes and demonstrate its dedication. Whereas, ease is non-confrontational, isn't interested in the problems, doesn't need to make any changes, and overall is easy-going and responsible. We are satisfied and confident in how far we've come and feel content to maintain status quo—nothing missing but also nothing improving either.

Therefore we are less concerned with trying to right any wrongs and would rather just let the world handle itself.

Our sense of power and self-esteem have begun to be internalized, and therefore whether we win or lose the competition doesn't really matter as much anymore. Ease therefore doesn't want to make any waves and is confident it will be okay no matter what happens. While it is nice to be at ease with life, we will eventually come to realize it is even more rewarding to *affirm* and *love* life back through self-motivated, inspired action.

Triggers That Keep Us Stuck Here

The theme of ease, if lingered in for too long, becomes the theme of complacency and can hinder further spiritual development. We may resort to resting in ease anytime there is confrontation or more effort required to go above and beyond the status quo. This is because we may feel exhausted from facing the challenges of life with courage and accountability, whether internally with our ego and past emotional wounds or with the world and other people. In the theme of ease we will crave rest, retirement, contentment, and will feel uninterested by the thought of having to keep putting more energy into our life.

Accompanying thoughts for the theme of ease are things like, "To each their own. I'm happy with what I have. I don't need to accomplish anything more. Where are you trying to get? Live and let live. It's none of my business. Arguing won't change anything. If this doesn't work out, something else will. Everything tends to be fine in the end. There's no need to get so worked up. Everyone just needs to relax and stop fighting. Trust in the goodness of life. Just go with the flow. There's nothing to fix. The world doesn't need fixing, we all just need to enjoy what we have been given. Looking for problems, creates problems. Just let it go."

Transcendence

Once we feel comfortable with this newfound ease and non-confrontational view of life, we can progress to even grander states of joy and expression of our true Self. We do this by seeing that when we voluntarily give more to life, it only seems to give back even more as well. While accountability participated out of duty and responsibility, the next stage of evolution is to participate with a willingness and self-motivation to share our gifts and talents out of gratitude and the joy of inspiration.

Thus eagerness to continue self-development for the sake of uplifting ourselves and others is more rewarding than maintaining the status quo. Through voluntary, inspired participation with life we get to enjoy even more self-esteem and the joys of succeeding at our ambitions. The theme of ease, therefore, is transcended through re-engagement with life, this time not out of any need or obligation but out of aspiration and excitement.

New Narrative

I want to be the best version of myself. I want to positively impact the world. What I do matters. I have something unique to give. I have talents to share that were given specifically to me. I uplift others. The more I give the more I enjoy. My involvement benefits the world. My dreams and ambitions were given to me for a reason. I have a unique purpose. I am motivated. I am inspired. I am needed. I am driven. My future is positive and bright. I can do anything I set my mind to. I am a success. My life is a success. I am talented. I am capable. Anything is possible. I have no limits except the ones I place on myself.

Self-Motivation at a glance

ARCHETYPE:
   The Overachiever

ROOT PROGRAM:
   Go above and beyond
   Explore full potential

TRIGGERS THAT KEEP US
STUCK HERE:
   Attachment to outcomes
   Unwilling to accept limits

PRIMARY EMOTION:
   Willingness

HOW TO ACCESS
THIS THEME:
   Ask what else is possible?
   Is this my potential?

WHAT IT'S WORKING ON:
   Exploring full potential
   Mastering talents/gifts
   Living as full as possible
   Self-esteem of achievement
   The more I give, the more
      I receive

MEDIA CHOICES:
   Doing the impossible
   Greatness/Hall of Fame
   Limitless Possibilities
   Mastery of a craft
   Wealth/success
   Inspirational

PHYSICAL
MANIFESTATIONS:
   Body's full health potential:
      how strong can I be?
   Heightened cognitive skills:
      how smart can I be?
   Wealth and success:
      how abundant can I be?
   Positive self-esteem
      through achievement

APPROACH TO
CHALLENGES:
  I can do anything I set
  my mind to

THOUGHTS/VALUES:
  Anything is possible
  Greatness is within me
  There are no limits
  Where there's a will, there's
  a way

TRANSCENDENCE:
  Full effort with
    acceptance of things
    beyond our control and
    non-attachment to results

AFFIRMATIONS TO
ASCEND:
  I can't control everything
  I am only responsible for
    my effort and intention
  Results/outcomes of my
    efforts are determined by
    infinite variables out of
    my control
  My worth is not determined
    from my results

Overview

When we embody the theme of self-motivation, the primary focus becomes that of enjoying and affirming life and therefore developing our self-esteem and exploring our unique gifts and talents. Resilience and the ability to handle delayed gratification strengthens, thus giving the theme of self-motivation the energy to seek positive change for itself and its loved ones, despite obstacles. We become willing and eager to improve ourselves, promote goodness and love, and tap into genuine inspiration. Success is common in all aspects of life since we now have access to true power that is able to go *above* and *beyond* the complacencies of our ego.

Through empowerment, ambition, and willingness to explore possibilities, there comes the ability to master increasingly sophisticated aspects of life such as our career, relationships, artistic pursuits, hobbies, academic performance, and anything else we're drawn towards. Previous to this theme of consciousness, positive action was taken out of obligation and sense of responsibility or to maintain status quo. Once the scale tips out of ease, however, the theme of self-motivation becomes interested in doing things to the best of its ability for the simple sake of enjoying what its capable of. We are excited to explore our abilities through opportunities to achieve, which we perceive all around us. We are enthusiastic and give 110% in all that we do. In this theme of consciousness, we no longer perceive our work, life obligations, or mundane tasks as a burden or duty but are grateful for the chance to demonstrate our unique gifts, talents, and greatness.

Everything is an exciting challenge and adventure and we are extremely confident in our ability to persevere and succeed.

Life is a blank canvas waiting for us to create, participate, and get involved in. The inner reward of enjoying our own achievements becomes the dominant motivating factor behind all action. It is the humble exploration of the gift of life and asks, "What am I capable of? How impactful can I become? What can I achieve and give to the world? What am I here to do? What else is possible?"

Happiness and satisfaction in our lives continues to become more internalized and our confidence swells with each new achievement. We show up to life fully engaged with a positive attitude and optimism. The theme of self-motivation is the epitome of ambitious entrepreneurship, passionate creativity, and driven self-esteem. Spiritually, it manifests as the devotee enjoying service to Divinity for positive karma, or merit, through selfless action, such as community or church service.

As a result of this newly awakened inner power, happiness is commonplace due to our ability to re-own control over our internal reality. Our zeal for achievement and the betterment of our lives and others makes us a positive power of change and inspiration.

When we examine the urge for self-motivation, it will be discovered to be coming from a place of needing to still earn *acceptance*, even if it is internal and subtle. This drive for acceptance leaves it vulnerable to periodic bouts with the limiting themes of desire, anger, or pride. While the invigoration and optimism of self-motivation is effulgent in comparison to themes previous to it, there is still so much more security to be explored on the journey to true freedom and lasting happiness.

Triggers That Keep Us Stuck Here

Although the theme of self-motivation is incredibly willing, inspired, and driven, it ultimately still has something to prove—even if it's to itself. Self-motivation, therefore, will be held back by attachment to aspirations and the need to achieve.

It will think things like, "Where there's a will, there's a way. I have a purpose (dharma) to fulfill. I can achieve anything I set my mind to. Anything is possible with enough dedication and hard work. Life is exciting and fun. Good things work out for me. Life is filled with opportunity. I have gifts to share. I am talented. I can learn anything I need to. I can be successful at anything I choose. I can develop any skills necessary. I am completely capable. I'd be wasting my life if I don't achieve my goals. I am here to achieve my mission. I have dreams to fulfill and manifest."

Transcendence

In order to transcend the limitations of self-motivation, we must accept that our intention for greatness, in and of itself, is enough. When attached to the theme of self-motivation, we may become overachievers and miss out on genuine self-acceptance and contentment. Our self-acceptance may always seem like one more achievement away, e.g., one more selfless act, one more community service project, one more degree, one more business, one more financial goal, etc. Spiritually, we may feel like our good deeds are never enough and so miss out on genuine forgiveness and the peace of accepting Divine Love. Thus we withhold acceptance and forgiveness from ourselves and others, not realizing that there is nothing to actually earn or forgive—only *accept what is freely given.*

To move forward, we must realize that our *striving* to be a good person *is* what makes us a good person, not any particular self-improvement achievement. There is no "perfection" to reach and then we will finally fully accept ourselves. Acceptance comes through showing up to each moment with our highest intentions and knowing that we will eternally be learning and growing—there is no fantasized "end" to attain. Thus to move beyond the limitations of self-motivation, we must see that our striving with full effort is enough and we can let go of attachment to the outcome. Equal parts effort. Equal parts non-attachment.

New Narrative

My desire to be a good person is what makes me one. My intentions are enough. I am only responsible for my effort. I accept myself as I am. I accept myself and others despite shortcomings. I accept myself with or without my accolades of achievement. I am always doing the best I can and that is all I can do. I am always exactly where I am supposed to be. I accept I am enough already. I am already forgiven. I am whole and complete and always have been. I am perfect just the way I am. I tried my best and that's all that matters. I am proud of myself no matter what the outcome. I always do my very best.

Acceptance at a glance

ARCHETYPE:

The Peacekeeper

TRIGGERS THAT KEEP US
STUCK HERE:

Aversion to understanding
for fear of it leading to
confrontation

HOW TO ACCESS
THIS THEME:

Have compassion for
the human condition

MEDIA CHOICES:

Forgiveness

Compassion for the
human condition

Humanitarianism

Peace and surrender

Self-acceptance

Kindness

ROOT PROGRAM:

I am enough
I don't need to know the
why or how

PRIMARY EMOTION:

Grace

WHAT IT'S WORKING ON:

Self-validation instead of
result driven validation

Compassion/forgiveness

Accepting limits of humans

Being present with what is

Non-attachment to results

PHYSICAL
MANIFESTATIONS:

Fully matured self-esteem:
self-validated

Extreme reduction of stress:
freedom from pressure to
perform as source of worth

Radiance

Vitality

APPROACH TO
CHALLENGES:
   100% effort *and also*
    100% non-attachment
    to results

THOUGHTS/VALUES:
   What I know is I don't
    know and that's okay
   I accept the limits of being
    human
   We are all doing the best we
    can with what we inherited
   All are worthy of
    forgiveness/compassion

TRANSCENDENCE:
   Seek to understand
    in order to serve others
    even more

AFFIRMATIONS TO
ASCEND:
   Understanding expands
    the ability to love others
   Knowledge benefits and
    serves humanity
   Understanding for the sake
    of benefiting others does
    not lead to confrontation
   Knowledge/Truth unites
    humanity

Overview

While the theme of self-motivation inspires us to prove our capabilities to ourselves and others, self-acceptance settles into emotional security and contentment by appreciating ourselves and others regardless of achievements. Acceptance releases expectations and is emotionally secure even when things don't work out despite all our effort and willingness. While ease is complacent in order to avoid confrontation, acceptance still puts forth the effort developed in the theme of self-motivation, but does so without the attachment to results. It is therefore entirely accepting of itself and others despite outcomes.

There comes a realization that we are only responsible for our own intentions and the rest is not up to us due to the infinite variables involved in any given situation. Thus nothing is perceived as lacking or unresolved within our self-esteem. Acceptance takes accountability for its happiness and doesn't blame other people or circumstances for how it feels. We accept our power to choose how we view our reality and what we believe.

We are therefore patient, forgiving, non-confrontational, and kind. Taking emotional positions breeds confrontation and the polarities of me vs. you, right vs. wrong, positive vs. negative, etc. Acceptance believes it is much more enjoyable to allow and accept life's diversity and trust in Divinity's perfect love.

Since we are all free to choose our own perceptions of our lives, other people and the world are viewed with respect and appreciation, and others' opinions are not taken personally. Acceptance sees the vast differences of human experience and lets go of judgment and admits it has no idea why things are the way they are but trusts and accepts that it is for a higher reason.

Triggers That Keep Us Stuck Here

Acceptance is always seeking balance, harmony, and compassion so it will have an aversion to any sort of confrontation, judgment, or pride. Its entire aim is always peace and for itself and others to feel seen, heard, and validated. It is the innocent wish that everyone could just get along and be kind and respectful to each other.

Acceptance affirms, "All is as it should be for reasons beyond my understanding. What I know is that I don't know—and that's okay. I accept myself and my life as it is. I don't need to know why or how. I only have control over my own life and allow all others the same freedom. I accept my limitations as a human and release all judgments. We are all doing the best we can with what we know. I forgive myself and others. Harmony is most important. Can't we just be at peace with each other and get along? There's no need for confrontation. We can't possibly understand something so complex. We are so limited in our understanding. We don't need to know the reasons. Trying to figure it out will only lead to judgment. I don't want to cause an argument. I prefer peace over being right."

Transcendence

Acceptance will have a subtle aversion to trying to understand the "why" or "how." This comes from the belief that needing to understand is synonymous with judgment or pride and will lead to confrontation—especially in the form of using knowledge as a form of power over others. This aversion to seeking to understand is blocking it from an even grander expression of the joy and love of life.

To transcend acceptance requires us to see that it is possible to enjoy contemplating the mysteries of life and accumulating knowledge without judgment and pride but instead curiosity, humility, and gratitude. If we take on the perspective of a true scientist, it is possible to explore the nature of things without getting drawn into the ego traps of being opinionated, confrontational, or power-seeking. Knowledge does not have to lead to attachment and pride if we relinquish credit-seeking.

When we enjoy learning about the "why" and "how" of life, it brings forth interest in complex data retention, science, medicine, invention, discovery, and understanding of human consciousness. While acceptance may create peace and harmony, moving into reason and logic creates further advancement and evolution of innovation for the betterment of all. Thus to explore the next stage of evolution requires acceptance to reinvest energy into the exploration of "What else is possible?" and begin to tap into our unique genius waiting to be manifested into the world.

New Narrative

Knowledge leads to greater gratitude and appreciation. I love learning new things. I tap into my genius that is *given* to me. I grow as I learn. Life becomes even more meaningful as I learn how it all works. Knowledge leads to awe. Inspired knowledge uplifts humanity. I seek to understand without judgment. Understanding brings wisdom and peace. With wisdom, I can be of greater service to myself and others. Understanding is to care and heal. I seek to understand myself and others with compassion. I am rational. I make wise choices with reason and logic. Rationality benefits myself and others. Reason and logic can transform the world through inspired invention and discovery. True knowledge can cure the suffering of the world. Understanding can bring greater peace to humanity.

Understanding at a glance

ARCHETYPE:

    The Scientist

ROOT PROGRAM:

    Understand and verify

TRIGGERS THAT KEEP US
STUCK HERE:

    Objectivity and knowledge

    Aversion to subjectivity

PRIMARY EMOTION:

    Composed

HOW TO ACCESS
THIS THEME:

    Seek to understand the truth

      without bias or opinion

WHAT IT'S WORKING ON:

    Understanding the "why"

      and "how" of things

    Letting go of bias and

      opinion to discover

      the truth of a matter

    Seeking knowledge to find

      solutions for suffering

MEDIA CHOICES:

    Documentaries

    Cerebral/Psychological

    Thought provoking

    Latest research

    Scientific

    Innovation and evolution

PHYSICAL
MANIFESTATIONS:

    Heightened IQ

    Peak brain performance

    Mastery of concentration

    Health optimization due to

      knowledge

APPROACH TO
CHALLENGES:
 Methodical, linear, planned
  researched, non-emotional

THOUGHTS/VALUES:
 Knowledge is power
 Science has all the answers
 Is it verifiable?
 Objective data
 Emotions are irrational

TRANSCENDENCE:
 Believe and have faith
 Trust in the power of love
 Open to the subjective
  mystery of life

AFFIRMATIONS TO
ASCEND:
 Objectivity is ultimately
  only experienced
  subjectively
 Subjectivity is the source of
  all conscious experience
 Consciousness precedes
  logic
 Faith and power of belief
  can trump logic
 Love is the wisest approach
  to life

Overview

Through taking emotional accountability over our lives, the mind feels secure enough to now become interested in understanding *how* and *why* things are the way they are. In the theme of understanding, there is a transcendence of the limiting themes of emotionalism and confirmation bias that block rational thinking and logical deduction beyond emotion and opinion. Thus, what is measurable, provable, and verifiable is of most interest, not just what the emotional, biased ego *assumes* or *wishes* was reality.

There evolves an attraction to anything developing the mind, such as research, academic study, science, medicine, and the accumulation of knowledge. It is the fascination with learning, objective analysis, causality, deduction, and the ability to process abstract concepts. The mind becomes enamored with itself and its ability "to think," which also opens the possibility to be tempted back into pride. Thus a downside of greater understanding is getting so preoccupied with the linear details of life and taking everything literally that it misses the point altogether—like getting lost overanalyzing the individual trees and missing the whole beauty of the forest.

We can note that all the wounded themes of consciousness are associated with the human-animal emotions: rejection and judgement of being ostracized by the pack, overwhelm of being abandoned to survive alone, grief over the loss of security, fight or flight from fear of death, desire to mate and survive, aggression and violence of competition, and pride of being the one who survives best and has the most "power." From the perspective of understanding, these themes of emotional insecurity are seen as a primitive inheritance of the reptilian brain within the human species. Because reason and logic view the animal emotions as an annoyance to rationality, our sense of self officially moves from attachment to the body and its emotions to the mind as "the thinker" of thoughts.

Everything from existence, the universe, the details of the world, societal governance, technology, to how the body and mind work all comes into question.

Who am I? Where did I come from? How does this all work? How did I get here? What is it all about? How do I exist? What is the universe made of? How does the body work? Why is the world the way it is? Why do I think what I think? Why do I do what I do? Why do I suffer? What is the most optimal way to experience life? What is the wisest thing to do here?

It is worth noting that reason and logic used with ulterior, ego motives stemming from a wounded theme of consciousness skews it to the destructive side. True understanding is a *gift* of enlightened thought that stems purely from Divinity. It can be either incredibly uplifting to society or entirely destructive, depending on how it is used. For example, reason and logic can be used to create nuclear weapons or cures for diseases and poverty. When used for the betterment of humanity, it is the highest form of human evolution within the physical plane, manifesting as the scientist, the doctor, the teacher, the statesmen, the inventive genius, etc. Devoid of pride and ego, all true genius is accompanied by humility and is admitted to not be personal—as all inventive or inspired breakthroughs are *gifts* from Divinity and *come through* us, not *from* us.

Genuine understanding is the realization of divine inspiration that manifests through the human mind in order to be used for the benefit of all life. Because of its double-edged sword nature, it must be used with the intention of relieving suffering and benefiting ourselves, humanity, other life forms, and the planet. Thus the theme of understanding finds solutions to humanity's woes. It invents to improve our lives, such as sewage systems and city planning, medicine and science, or technology that create convenience, such as cars, planes, and computers. It creates systems of governing and education and strives to help others in whichever field it manifests.

Triggers That Keep Us Stuck Here

While overall this is the theme of all scientific geniuses, the theme of understanding's downside is the attachment to the mind and its thoughts as "mine," subsequently leading to the ego's vanity of "*I* know." The deduction of the intellect is, "I think, therefore I am," whereas the realization of the spirit is, "I am." Thus intellectual pride and attachment to thinking as the source of survival resurface as the primary barrier to further evolution into the liberating themes of *Spiritual Reality*. This theme will therefore be triggered and held back by a preoccupation with details, facts, objectivity, causality, and the need for verifiable proof—unable to believe or have faith in something beyond itself that it can't objectively measure.

Accompanying thoughts of the theme of understanding will be things like, "*I* know. *I* think. Knowledge is power. Education is essential. Can you prove it? Is it verifiable? What is the evidence? I know this based on my studies and results. I don't believe that.

Faith is only wishful thinking. If it can't be measured, it is not verifiable. I am skeptical if it can't be proven. How does this work? Why is it this way? Let's test it. Show me the data. What are the facts? Do they have a degree? I only trust experts. What are their credentials? Is it peer-reviewed? Love and companionship are a rational, societal utility. Don't be emotional. Intuition can't be trusted. Emotions are irrational. Be rational. Be logical. What's the most logical choice? It has to make sense."

Transcendence

The mind cannot transcend reason and logic because the mind is too attached to objective verification and therefore cannot comprehend a subjective, Spiritual Reality. The transcendence of this theme only comes from looking *beyond* the linear mind for greater truth. Spiritual realization is not something objectively proven; it can only be *experienced* as an internal, invisible shift in conscious awareness.

Another major hindrance to transcendence is the mind's vanity and pride. The mind attached to understanding takes all the credit for its thoughts and believes itself to be its own source of existence. Due to this, the mind can't comprehend trusting something beyond itself for survival. Thus it cannot see that all of life is a continuous *gift* and that its thoughts have never actually been coming from a "me." Every moment of life is a gift, all of our thoughts and inspirations are gifts. "From who or what?" is the question that we must ponder.

This transition can only be *invited* and *surrendered to* through the spiritual will. Consciousness, as the spiritual source of existence, thus reveals itself as that which is totally obvious but has simply been overlooked because it is radically subjective. Up until this point, our reliance on the dualistic perceptions of reason and logic have blocked us from accepting how unexplainable our existence is to begin with. We are so busy looking "out there," we forget that we actually exist "in here."

As the theme of understanding continues to explore this newfound internal reality, we discover consciousness is actually influencing all experience of objectivity. The external reality we experience is determined by our inner reality. The themes of consciousness entirely influence our perceptions of the physical world. Each theme is only able to perceive that which is within its paradigm of possibility. Objectivity is, therefore, in the eyes of the beholder.

Rationality concludes that this ability to choose perception of our physical reality is absolutely fundamental to what determines our quality of life. Thus to weave a narrative about ourselves, Divinity, and the world from the perspectives of a wounded theme will bring the consequence of those types of thoughts and feelings. And likewise, to endorse a higher, liberating theme of perspective on our lives, we enjoy the consequences of those types of thoughts and feelings as well. The question then becomes, "What is the most logical, wise perspective?" Which inevitably leads us to love.

New Narrative

All thoughts are impersonal. I am not my thoughts. I am that which is observing my thoughts. My life is a gift from something beyond my understanding. All the answers are *given* to me. My heart knows more than my mind. I believe and have faith. I believe in the goodness of life. Just because I can't comprehend it doesn't mean it isn't real. There is so much more than meets the eye. There are entire spiritual realities beyond my limited perception. I rely on belief and faith to guide me. Some things can't be explained. Love is the most logical choice. Consciousness is all there is. I surrender to something Higher. I open myself up to the great mystery of Creation. Divinity is the source of my existence. I trust that I'm always being guided. Reality is subjective. There is unlimited possibility and potential. I am a spiritual being having a human experience.

Chapter 11

True Freedom & Lasting Happiness

"Faith sees the invisible, believes the unbelievable,
and receives the impossible."
- Corrie ten Boom

R elying on faith is either a stopping point in our evolution of consciousness or through the invitation of our spiritual will, the soul steps forward as the new source of grander truth and our sense of identity. This consequently unlocks an entire level of existence never before considered.

While the theme of understanding represents the most evolved theme of consciousness within physical reality, it is ultimately still missing out on access to the true freedom and lasting happiness which comes from acknowledging a spiritual reality. Without a spiritual context of reality, the logical mind is limited and cannot enjoy the bliss of trusting in a Divinity beyond itself. Thus it will always be haunted by the ultimate fear of death and the unknown of going beyond the physical. All themes of consciousness previous to a Spiritual Reality could be characterized as seeing the body and mind as the source of consciousness (existence), whereas the themes past this point view consciousness as the source of our experiences of the body and mind. Consciousness is beyond time and space and who we really are, our true Self, while the human body and mind are passing expressions within it. The perceived universe is more so being projected from *within* us rather than something we are separate from. The universe we perceive only exists within our own consciousness and is relative to our theme of consciousness. We all are perceiving different layers or dimensions of reality. From a grander, non-dualistic perspective, even the notions of "inner" and "outer," "this" and "that," or subject and object begin to merge and eventually are realized to all be one and the same. Such a realization is beyond reason and leads into the realms of the mystical and nonlinear.

As much as it resists the unexplainable power of belief, the mind is forced to surrender to the fact that belief and faith actually dictate our experience of reality. This power of belief is most obviously demonstrated through the placebo effect and its defiance of reason and logic. The placebo effect is the phenomenon of giving a patient something that has no actual medicinal value, but the patient's *faith* and *belief* in its healing abilities create an actual healing effect physiologically. Logically speaking, this should be impossible and yet it happens frequently enough that it has to be taken into consideration whenever introducing a new medical innovation or treatment. This is just one of countless examples of the miraculous and mysterious power of belief and further demonstrates that belief and faith trump reason and logic by methods that it can't explain or measure.

At this incredible tipping point, consciousness—our unexplainable spiritual essence—has officially been accepted as our identity, and we loosen our attachment on the external world. It is at this point in our journey we transition out of self-mastery and into the mystery. The realization of our spiritual nature brings with it exquisite, unlimited access to love and peace that is able to transcend physical circumstances. While the human ego lives in constant existential insecurity because of the inevitability of physical death, the spirit lives in the realms of true freedom and lasting happiness because it is eternal and therefore its existence is *already guaranteed.*

THEMES OF ENLIGHTENMENT

5D Reality

Self As Spirit

ECSTASY

Unity Mentality

FREEDOM &
HAPPINESS

LOVE &
INNER PEACE

SPECTRUM OF ENLIGHTENMENT

0 = NEVER | 1 = RARELY | 2 = SOMETIMES | 3 = OFTEN | 4 = CONSISTENTLY

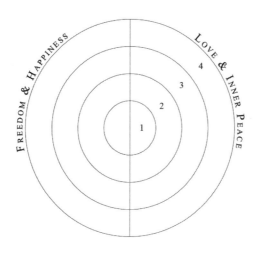

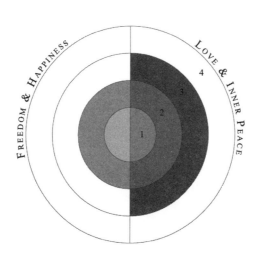

Love & Inner Peace at a glance

ARCHETYPE:
 The Saint

ROOT PROGRAM:
 I am the source of love,
   peace, and happiness

TRIGGERS THAT KEEP US
STUCK HERE:
 Conditional love and
  attachment to preferences

PRIMARY EMOTION:
 Gratitude & Serenity

WHAT IT'S WORKING ON:
 Loving self and others
 Being peaceful within and
  uplifting others
 Creating the most loving
  world
 Connecting with Divinity
  as ultimate source of love

HOW TO ACCESS
THIS THEME:
 Ask how can my thoughts
  and actions benefit myself
  and others the most?

MEDIA CHOICES:
 Uplifting, inspiring
 Devotional
 Loving and peaceful
 Spiritual—God as love

PHYSICAL
MANIFESTATIONS:
 Ultimate wellness and
  vitality
 Radiance and inspiration
 Spontaneous healing

APPROACH TO
CHALLENGES:
  Inspired, trusting, prayer
    go within, listen and look
    for signs, intuitive

THOUGHTS/VALUES:
  Love is the path to all
    fulfillment and happiness
  Love can do the miraculous
  Divine Love is the source
    of all existence
  Life is a gift of ultimate love
  Love is the source of all
    inspiration and goodness
    in the world

TRANSCENDENCE:
  Unconditional love through
    release of attachment
    to preferences
  Full surrender to trust in
    Divine Love

AFFIRMATIONS TO
ASCEND:
  Unconditional love allows
    for free will
  From an eternal perspective
    everything is leading
    to greater love eventually
  My preferences are just
    one expression of love
  Love also comes in disguise
    in the form of growth and
    wisdom learned through
    hardships

Overview

With the dawning of spiritual awakening emerges the opportunity to access love and peace from the eternal spring *within*. Inner peace is experienced as the natural consequence of finally remembering the truth of our spiritual nature and finding gratitude beyond circumstances. Therefore if all subjective states are an inner choice of perspective, it would only make sense to choose to see our existence from a perspective that evokes happiness, gratitude, love, and fulfillment. And as we align with our highest version of lovingness, it only benefits ourselves and others, therefore only perpetuating itself.

It is worth noting that what the world considers love is typically referring to infatuation, possessiveness, pride, or desirous attachment. True love is *embodied* and a lifestyle approach. As we move into the frequency of love, we become aware of the love and goodness that is all around us; we just didn't recognize it before. True love doesn't need a reason to love; it just loves because that is its nature.

In the theme of love and inner peace, we start to finally experience the highest potentials of human reality. Everything can be perceived with love if we stretch ourselves beyond the linear mind's parameters. It's as if we are seeing the world for the first time, and in many ways, we are. Colors appear more vibrant; we notice the dewy leaves glistening in the sunlight as if revealing a glorious painting; bumblebees are no longer a nuisance but instead become messengers giving us their blessing. We notice recurring numbers sensing they carry a meaning and license plates stand out, giving us signs. Nothing is just mundane or ordinary anymore. The trees are now dancing for us; the flowers are blooming just to show us how beautiful they are. Everything seems to be in synchronistic harmony. Everywhere we look we see the magic of Divine Love and life is forever transformed into heaven on earth through the newly discovered lenses of love. The irony is the world didn't change; we did.

In the frequency of love everything has meaning and purpose and is communicating loving guidance to us, including our current situation and circumstances. Every challenge, or life situation, becomes an opportunity for further spiritual awakening. Every perceived setback becomes a redirection by Divinity for our growth. There are no more accidents or coincidences. Everything becomes a part of the cosmic dialogue between the Creator and us. Love perceives a loving universe, and everything can be viewed with a positive angle. Even when the meaning or purpose of an event in our lives is yet to be understood, we easily give it over to hope and faith, trusting that it will be revealed to us in due time.

Because consciousness is vibrating in the frequency of love, it sees love everywhere it looks. As mentioned before, even debt is not an enemy of love. Love thinks, "Thank you God for providing me a way to get ahead and for providing me the way to pay this back tenfold. My future must be really bright!" If it has perceived competition in work or confrontations in the world, it thinks, "Thank you God for providing me the opportunity to surrender, forgive, and exercise my faith in goodness. All is as it should be. What will be, will be. If this opportunity wasn't meant for me, it only means something *even better* is coming."

From the perspective of love, we realize that all beings are an embodiment of a theme of consciousness, and therefore what others bring forth only demonstrates *their* current nature, not our own. Hence the teaching, *by their fruits you shall know them*. If all experience of life is based on an internal narrative, then that means that nothing is intrinsically objective or personally offensive in life. For example, even when targeted by anger, hate, or slander, it is only a projection of another's internal reality. All suffering is self-created through limiting root programs. This is why great spiritual teachers taught, *pray for your enemies because they bring themselves down by their own hand.*

These realizations allow us not to take the suffering of the world personally, which would just make us fall back into limitation ourselves. Instead, we have immense empathy, compassion, and patience for the shadow side of humanity. Love respects everyone's own unique journey through the darkness. To any perceived adversary, love says, "Thank you for the opportunity to forgive and learn about myself. How can I help you out of your suffering? I see you. I understand you are hurting. I love you." Thus compassion towards all life becomes the natural response in this theme.

There is nothing love can't find gratitude for. Life is a gift, and most of it is out of our control. What we do seem to have control over though, is our perspective *of* this gift of life. Therefore the most loving perspective to take is that all is exactly as it should be, is unfolding for the greatest good, and that there is no need to judge or change anything. All is perfect as it is without accident, mistake, or coincidence. There is perfect justice, balance, and harmony that we may not be able to see with our limited human perspective, but we trust in the perfect consequences of Creation that may stem vastly beyond this lifetime. Through believing and having faith in such perspectives, we notice dramatic increases in our overall levels of internal freedom, joy, and inner peace.

All of love's existence is beautiful, hopeful, and based in radical faith. Doubt, worry, fear, anger, expectations, regret, pride, and greed are all things of the past because they are no longer attractive as a viable option. In love, there is enough to go around. Love isn't concerned with what it can get, but what it can give. In this state of consciousness, there is no longer fear of lack. And love wants to show graciousness and abundance to anyone suffering from this fear in hopes that they too, will come to realize the generosity of the universe.

Love moves beyond the physical realm and perceives energy and essence through intuition. Before the transition into spiritual reality, we might focus on linear details such as words, actions, facial expressions, voice inflection and tone, body language, or even someone's appearance when interacting. But when love interacts with another being, it is primarily experiencing their subjective energy or essence (theme of consciousness). It is the difference between seeing versus an intuitive *knowing*.

Triggers That Keep Us Stuck Here

In the early onset of this theme, we must be aware of preferences creating a subconscious hierarchy around things we find beautiful and divine. Conditional love is a trigger for this theme as it only experiences love in certain things, but not necessarily *all* things *yet*. This limitation is something to process and release in order to realize true freedom and lasting happiness beyond preferences.

Someone in love will commonly think things like, "What a glorious life! Life is such an amazing gift! How beautiful _____ is!

Thank you Creator for all my countless blessings. I don't know why this is happening, but one day it'll all make sense. There is a higher reason for everything, even if it is beyond my understanding right now. I don't know why this didn't work out for me, but it must be guiding me to something *even better*. I have faith. I believe in the goodness of life. I have compassion and love for others. I choose to see the good in everyone. I have hope. I choose to surround myself with positive people and energy. They know not what they do. I distance myself from negativity. I have healthy boundaries. I love my life. I am at peace with whatever happens. Everything is working out for my benefit. How can I help you? What joy can I contribute to this situation?"

Transcendence

To go from conditional to unconditional love we have to expand our awareness of love to even include all that we would typically deem "unlovable," "tragic," or "ugly" in the world. This final step into true freedom and lasting happiness moves beyond preferences altogether. Instead, we explore the innocence of consciousness—which includes *everything in existence*. Unconditional love sees that our preferences are not better than our not-preferences. All things are equally divine for simply existing and are a reflection of the infinite possibilities of Creation.

Unconditional love is only realized by letting go of the mind's attachments to hierarchies of dualities. "This" versus "that." Lovable versus unlovable. Happiness versus suffering. Positive versus negative. Life versus death. Best versus worst. Attachment to preferences will always place conditions on love and keep it limited due to the perception of a hierarchy between two opposing polarities. So long as something could be "better" than "this," the ego will always be able to create suffering through resistance to *what is—free of all preference or opinion.*

In order to be free from the bondage of dualities, we have to see that it is all *one—nonduality*. Everything in existence is all Divinity. It is all the same One; the ego just creates the illusion of separation because of its preferences and attachments. Thus it is not that we develop the ability to love the "unlovable"—we simply let go of the notion of unlovability in the first place. All labels are fallacious and come from an arbitrary, ego perspective. Beyond the labeling of preference, all is actually *perfect as is*. Nothing to say —ineffable.

In a unified, interconnected universe of innate consequence, all is exactly how it's supposed to be without possible accident, mistake, or error. To resist otherwise is to fight the entire universe being what it is. The limited ego resists love and focuses on all the proof for how *unloved* it is, whereas spirit focuses on all the proof for how *loved* it is. Both perspectives will technically feel "right" and justified, but the experience and consequences of each will be drastically different. All humanity could be in utter bliss of existence in an instant if we all accepted this effortless choice. For it is absolute bliss to live knowing all is perfectly aligned by Divine Love and not a single hair is out of place. All we must do is surrender resistance and accept it. Everyone has access to Divine Unconditional Love; nothing is being withheld.

True freedom and lasting happiness is the state of finally returning *home* to utter security, bliss, joy, love, peace, gratitude, and ineffable awe. Whatever it took to realize the truth of Divine Unconditional Love is seen as irrelevant and worth the cost. For, if that's what it took to bring us to this moment now, then it was perfect and exactly what our consciousness needed to awaken. All of us are on our perfect journey of remembering just how loved we are by Divinity. To exist is to already be utterly loved beyond comprehension. Yet, we seem to enjoy the hero's journey through the relativity of *not knowing*. Thus we explore all that is of our *not-Self* only to return to what was always there; we just didn't see it *yet*.

Unconditional love compassionately understands that some souls need to wander into dark confusions of shame and guilt in order to prove that they are still infinitely loved, while others accept it more readily and avoid the temptations of the ego's defiance of Divinity. Either way, it is all perfect and only revealing what is *eternally available to all*. However, Divine Love does not force itself and will only be noticed when *invited*. Hence this writing is an *invitation* to true freedom and lasting happiness.

New Narrative

All is love. All is Divine. All is perfect. All is Self. All is equally lovable just for existing. Divinity is in everything and everyone. Preferences are only coming from the ego. Nothing is better or worse. There is only eternal existence. There is no such thing as death. The void is an illusion and not an actual reality. Consciousness is all there is. All experience is within my consciousness, and my consciousness is pure love. Consciousness is free to choose to accept love or to reject it. I can choose to accept eternal love.

True Freedom & Lasting Happiness

Archetype:	*The Mystic*
Root Program:	*All is Love, All is Divine, All is Perfect*
Primary Emotion:	*Transcendence & Bliss*

What if everything is working out in the absolute best way it possibly could for you *right now*? What if *this* is your dream life? What if Divine Love is talking to you right now, reminding you to accept how loved you are? What if life is constantly guiding you? What if you could enjoy a life full of utter bliss and fulfillment *right now*?

As we explore the theme of love and inner peace, it naturally becomes unconditional by its very nature. As we consistently invite love and inner peace through disciplining our spiritual will, we gradually experience them in *all* things. Eventually perpetuating their continuance to the point of utter bliss. As we devote ourselves to actualizing true freedom and lasting happiness, every hidden attachment to past wounds that we may still struggle with arises to be healed and transcended through our spiritual devotion to choose differently.

Thus the acceptance of true freedom and lasting happiness requires **accountability** to face our hidden attachments and wounds, seeing our ego inheritance with the impartiality of **ease, self-motivation** to exercise discipline to see our *Inner Work* through, **acceptance** that all is as it should be for reasons unknown to us, **understanding** to see love as the wisest and most enjoyable approach to life, and as we embody **love and inner peace** it evolves into unconditional ***true freedom and lasting happiness***.

This emergence of true freedom and lasting happiness is the dawning of Self-realization. The ecstatic bliss that all great teachers have been pointing humanity to. However, the awakening of our true Self is not about creating another alter, spiritual ego. The ego does not become enlightened. The ego does not become the true Self. Instead, the true Self is *revealed* as we shed attachment *to* the ego by turning away from its opinions and limitations of reality. We discover the Self within others is revealed to be the same Self within us, and all existence shines forth as a glorious, unexplainable Creation of the Divine "I".

When consciousness expands to this level of awareness, we see our lives as a continuous expression of Divinity. Our sense of personal will eventually dissolves into the Divine Will, and it is as if we are watching a movie from the eyes of an avatar body—*the Divine Reality*. The body just goes about its business according to its destiny and plays the role it's supposed to play within the grand scheme of things. The words just come out, inspirations arise when necessary, the body runs itself, and life flows effortlessly, all without attachment to a sense of "me" doing anything. We exist in the eternal *now,* and the state of *presence* becomes our every waking moment. All of life is a glorious, ineffable Creation of the Most High.

All of existence is rich with gratitude, appreciation, and silent awe that may or may not be expressed. At first, the radiance of awakening to such a blissful state is overwhelming; tears of joy may be common. But as the state ripens, it eventually settles into an inner awareness that transcends expression and is an inner tranquility of eternal satisfaction. The highs and lows, the suffering and the joy, the pain and the pleasure, all of it is seen as a divine experience of relativity. Therefore creating the joy of a hero's journey, giving meaning, purpose, and a sense of wondrous exploration to human life. True freedom and lasting happiness comes from awakening to the realization that it is not the perception of opposites that is the source of our suffering; it is our attachment to them being real that is causing us to "fall" from Eden.

From a higher perspective, it is actually all the same Self. There are no actual opposites, or dualities, that contend with each other, only the perception of such that the human mind created. For example, there is only Divine Love or rejection of it, which the mind has labeled as "evil." But this labeling process of the mind has created the illusion of something actually separate from Divine Love, which is only a mental projection. There is only Divinity, or rejection of Divinity. There is nothing actually separate from Divinity. Likewise, there is only true freedom and lasting happiness or rejection of it; suffering does not exist in and of itself. Human suffering is the consequence of adopting a limited perspective of our circumstances and becoming attached and identified with them. Finally, there is only eternal existence or denial and rejection of it. "Death" or nonexistence is only an imagination of the mind—not an actual reality. To exist, is to exist *always*.

Notice in all these examples there is only one variable that we either accept or reject. And so it is with the Divine mystery—one Self that is only being perceived as separate out of choice. All perceptions of dualities and perceived opposites are just arbitrary points on a spectrum of awareness that humanity accidentally mistook as actual realities. Therefore as we awaken to true freedom and lasting happiness, we finally can affirm that there is only freedom and happiness, only love and Divinity, only eternal existence. All perceptions otherwise are just layers of resistance to the Truth.

Unconditional love and nonduality *is* the consciousness of true freedom and lasting happiness. It is completely liberated from attachment to the wounded themes of consciousness, and its experience of life is truly Heaven within—the Garden of Eden restored. Everything is lovable, and everything is seen as divinely perfect *just for existing*. All existence is permeating with silent bliss. All the happiness, love, and fulfillment we have been searching for our entire life is eternally realized. There can be no more resistance, nothing could ever be wrong or out of place, all is forgiven, all is accepted, all is finally understood as an extension of the same Divine Self. We see that we are one with All That Is.

> *"I and the Father are one."*
> *- Holy Bible, John 10:30*

As unconditional love becomes a permanent state of being, we embody a saintly energy and are constantly emulating loving frequencies of peace and harmony to all of life regardless of if it seems to be the most 'tragic' or the most 'blessed.' Our circumstances may not even change at this point, we could have the same bills, same job, same relationships, but yet our view of them will be forever transformed as the bliss of our life is realized to be completely internal. Yet, it is worth noting that as our internal world shifts, our external world usually changes with it. The difference now, however, is that changing the external circumstances won't be the goal or focus anymore. True freedom and lasting happiness is the ultimate state of Grace, for all of life is loved, appreciated, and admired without measure or possible restraint. All humanity is capable of this realization; in fact, it is our inevitable destiny.

All things of love, joy, peace, and freedom are based in the truth of the Divine. All things based in negativity, control, or force are limiting, which is to say, based in ego delusions and to be avoided because they bring unpleasant consequences. Intuition and inner honesty are significant tools to be used to align us with our highest life purpose and keep us safe. Thus the caveat that needs to be known at the onset of this phase is that while everything may appear lovable to us, this does not mean that everyone else is in the same state. There still is a need for spiritual discernment of the themes of consciousness in order to make sure the innocent bliss of this state is not taken advantage of due to naivety. For example, you can love and appreciate a wild scorpion but also respect that it is safe to keep your distance. This is the difference between naive innocence and wise innocence—the difference between the child and the sage.

Follow the heart always and there can be no possible error. Our intuition does not lie, however the mind can be misled. All guidance will be revealed if we have the eyes to see and ears to hear. Have faith, trust the Divinity that sustains your existence, and know that all will be provided. You are always being guided to exactly where you're supposed to be and doing exactly what you're supposed to be doing. Consistently surrender any resistance to every moment, trusting that Divine Love is in control and *with you always*. There is nothing to figure out, nothing to contend with, nothing to earn, only surrender and trust in the goodness of life. What if everything is working out for the absolute best? Allow it to be revealed to you, and it will be so.

The Final Surrender

Transitioning into nonlinear spiritual reality requires letting go of belief systems that our mind has been reinforcing our entire lifetime. To let them go now seems absolutely foolish to the ego-mind. It tries to convince us, "I've kept us alive this whole time; why would you abandon me now? I'm the reason for all your progress. You're being irresponsible. If you stop listening to me, you will die without me. I *am* you. I've been doing all these things for us. I'm your best friend. I've been thinking all these plans and keeping us safe from enemies. I keep you alive. You can't trust or believe in anything other than me. It's dangerous if you don't listen to me. You're being irrational. You *need* me."

To go beyond the ego as the source of our life is to consciously accept the notion of death and face the existential fear of a perceived end. The ego can only imagine death as a void of nothingness, whereas the true Self experiences death as only a transition. From the perspective of a Spiritual Reality, what we call "death" is no different than waking up each morning.

> *"Try to imagine what it will be like to go to sleep*
> *and never wake up...*
> *now try to imagine what it was like to wake up*
> *having never gone to sleep."*
> *- Alan Watts*

Yet because what happens after death cannot be reported, proven, and verified through objective experimentation, the ego refuses to step into absolute faith and belief in a spiritual, eternal reality. The irony of the ego is that it actually already lives by faith and doesn't realize it—*faith that it knows anything at all*. Further still is the realization that the ego itself is an illusory identity that we innocently mistook as who we really were, like the actor getting lost in their role. Now, having traversed and released attachment to the themes of consciousness through practicing *The Inner Work*, we return to our original state of Satchitananda—*existence, consciousness, bliss*. No longer attached to the mind and body as "me" but rather as expressions of Creation. From the perspective of true freedom and lasting happiness, all has been unfolding of its own, and all we were responsible for was the intention and invitation to have the Truth revealed. The final surrender requires us to sincerely admit, "I *don't* know how I exist," which opens the door to Self-realization.

What if time itself is an illusion? What if there is no actual start and end? What if existence is actually beyond time and space? What if eternity is *right now*? What if all perception of duality and a physical universe is a holographic projection within the unnamable, unexplainable essence of our existence—*Consciousness*? What if there are no separations actually possible? What if love is something we can trust in and give our survival over to? What if Divinity is real and the only reason we exist at all? And what if that Divinity is the epitome of infinite, unconditional, ineffable *love* and *goodness*? What if the mind has never actually been doing or "thinking" anything, and all things have been *given*? What if there is an unnamable essence of goodness and infinite love that is pervading the entire universe and is the very core of our being—guiding all things? What if the best-case scenario was true, and life is a glorious expression of perfect love and goodness? What if we are all *one with* Divinity as an extension and expression of the Most High? What if Divinity is speaking to us *now*, inviting us to accept our Spiritual Reality? What if there were nothing to do, nothing to forgive, nothing to heal? What if we are liberated *now*?

Awakening Humanity

Once we realize the eternal bliss of true freedom and lasting happiness, the only thing left to do is to *invite* and *share* it with others that are seen as expressions of the same Self. Thus to love and heal others is to only love and heal ourselves. Which is why this writing comes forth as a loving *invitation*. So that all may have the opportunity to *remember* the bliss and joy of true freedom and lasting happiness. We invite you to extend this same invitation to everyone you know and love, so that all humanity may decide for themselves to put down their struggle with life and wake up to the glory of their divine existence. Ultimately there is no need, rush, and nothing to be forced. Within an eternal reality all is exactly as it should be and always in perfect "timing." The invitations of love we extend to the world are simply out of the joy of *giving* and *serving*.

Lokah Samastah Sukhino Bhavantu

"May all beings everywhere be happy and free, and may the thoughts, words, and actions of my own life contribute in some way to that happiness and to that freedom for all."

Living The Inner Work

As you do your *Inner Work*, your spectrum of consciousness will continue to change and evolve to reflect less energy being spent in the wounded themes and more energy being consistently expressed in the liberating themes. Continue to return to this book as a guide anytime you fall away from Truth. We recommend evaluating your current spectrum of consciousness often.

If you prefer a printable spectrum of consciousness, you can download a copy at theinnerwork.com/media

SPECTRUM OF CONSCIOUSNESS

0 = NEVER | 1= RARELY | 2 = SOMETIMES | 3= OFTEN | 4 = CONSISTENTLY

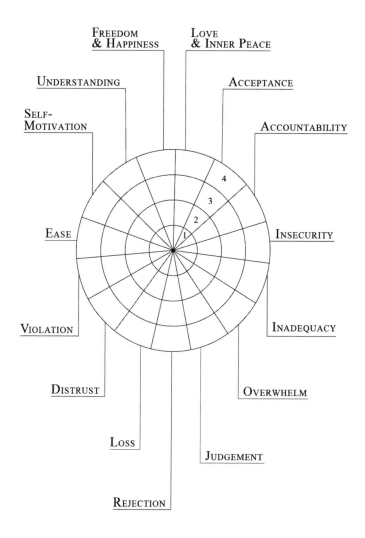

About the Authors

Mat & Ash are best known as The Yoga Couple ™ to their 1.5M+ online community. A devoted married couple, holistic healers, and modern spiritual teachers, their down to earth approach to Eastern philosophy and Western psychology makes spirituality and self-healing accessible to all. They are best-selling authors of *The Inner Work*, hosts of The Inner Work podcast, founders of Sacred Yoga Institute and live on the Big Island of Hawaii where they host retreats, trainings, and offer holistic counseling.

To learn more about Mat & Ash,

upcoming events, retreats, or trainings

visit theyogacouple.com

Follow Mat & Ash on Social Media:

Instagram: @TheYogaCouple

TikTok: @TheYogaCouple

YouTube: @TheYogaCouple

Facebook: @TheYogaCouple

You're Invited to a FREE
Inner Work Online Challenge

Includes BONUS videos and actionable growth activities!

Reading The Inner Work is a profound step in your self-healing journey. To support you in *doing* your Inner Work rather than just reading about it, we have designed a free interactive challenge to accompany your daily reading.

What's included in The Inner Work challenge:

• Inner Work Yoga Classes: Emotions are stored in the body. Learn how to somatically release stuck emotions through yoga, breathwork, and energy clearing practices. Each class is specifically designed to help address the themes of consciousness that you will learn in this book.

• Self-reflection activities: Receive actionable practices, guided meditations, journal prompts, podcast recordings, and Inner Work processes in your inbox.

• Exclusive Reader Community: Join our private online group to ask questions, share, and reflect with other Inner Workers.

By committing to The Inner Work Challenge, you're not just reading a book; you're actively integrating what you are learning and transforming yourself from the inside out

Answer The Call and Unlock This Free Gift:

theinnerwork.com/challenge

Help us share The Inner Work
with the world!

If this book has helped you or added value to your life we would be so grateful for you to take a moment to leave a review. As authors, it means so much to us to hear how The Inner Work has impacted your life and your review helps share and spread The Inner Work with the world!

Other ways you can help share
The Inner Work:

- Give this book to a friend

- Buy a copy as a gift for someone you love

- Share on social media. We love to see your photos and videos about The Inner Work.
Tag us @theinnerwork on all platforms

- Become an affiliate. Get a 15% commission for every book you sell online or on social media

Share The Inner Work with others:

theinnerwork.com/share